WHEN LOVE IS NOT ENOUGH

Chronicles of LauraJo

By
Pat Engebrecht

Also by Pat Engebrecht

Under the Haystack
Promise of Moonstone

Music: I have selected the following songs from a tape created for me by my daughter, LauraJo in 1983. These songs were composed and sung by her during her years of medical treatment for Borderline Personality Disorder (BPD).

Which Way to Turn
By LauraJo Engebrecht

Lonely with no where to go
Caught in the whirlwind of time
Tell me please which way must I
Turn to find some reason to find
Some rhyme.

Which way is up on this carousel of
Life spinning round 'till I can't see
The sky.
Try as I may I just can't see an end
Yet I know I must not cease to try.

Take my hand, be with me through
This storm, I can't seem to make it
Alone.
I know I said I could do it myself, but
I was wrong, Please take me home.

Which way is up on this carousel of life
Spinning round 'till I can't see the sky
Try as I may, I just can't see an end
Yet I know I must not cease to try,
Yes, I know I must not cease to try.

To my husband, Ron, and sons: Kurt and Jeff, who walked in the shadows loving LauraJo all the way.

To Dr. Cecile Carson, whose love allowed her to think outside the box.

To the many professionals who worked toward solving "The Problem": Dr. B. Kumetat, Dr. W. Scarborough, Dr. J. Sobel, Dr. G. Pleune, and many unnamed doctors who reached out to LJ.

To the many nurses: Pat, Carol, Pam, and other unnamed caretakers, who listened and gave their love and advice, but mostly their hearts.

To her friends along the way who lit her journey with the light of love: Stephanie, Sharon, Boothy, Suzanne, Dottie, Judy, and those I did not know.

And lastly, to parents who love **when love is not enough.**

A Dreamer
By LauraJo Engebrecht

After you're gone and the hollows of
My soul open to swallow the night.
I look to tomorrow and all it will
Bring and I struggle to keep you
In sight.

You're an angel, a dreamer, my friend
And my home and all that I want is to
Make you my own…my own.

Not the hours together but the moment
You smiled
Tells me I need you, I love you.
Your hair the sun shining on a summer's
Golden field, all that is beauty is you.

You're an angel, a dreamer, my friend
And my home and all that I want is to make
You my own…my own.

Stronger than a summer's storm
Gentle like a child—existing before yesterday
Long before we ever smiled you said come
In now and for a while will you stay.

You're an angel, a dreamer, my friend and my
Home and all that I want is to make you
My own…my own.

Author's Note

This book was written by a mother who has no *credentials* and certainly did not know the *territory.* I traveled through the abyss with a daughter lost in the limbo of medical ignorance, misunderstanding, and a variety of misdiagnoses, finally settling on the mental disorder still wrapped in the shrouds of mystery: *Borderline Personality Disorder.*

LauraJo, you gave your journals to Dr. Carson in hopes they might be of some help to the medical professionals treating BPD and other mental illness victims. After a year Dr. Carson returned them to me. I moved them around from home to home for over twenty years before I found the courage to reenter the years of grief, struggle and pain of your suffering, LJ. I have selected the entries to show your wholeness, not just your disease. Your comment on Page 65 has given me the freedom to show your private thoughts, *"...I don't care if someone reads it someday because when I look back on this I want to see the truth, all of it not half."* Your hopes have come true. Dr. Rachel Jordan, Professor of Advanced Mental Health Counseling at St. John

Fisher College in Rochester, N.Y. has selected **When Love is Not Enough Chronicles of LauraJo** as a text for her class. Your words live on.

Suicide: How does any parent survive such a death of their child? When the medical profession proclaims the major cause of BPD to be poor parenting, abuse (physical/sexual) neglect or abandonment, it is an indictment beyond recovery. I refuse to accept such a proclamation. I search for an answer turning back through the pages of my memory.

The images included have been retrieved from twenty-year-old scrap books and journals.

We Can
By LauraJo Engebrecht

Does anyone out there feel like me
So desperate and all alone.
Does it seem like you'll never find
A place that feels like home.

When the sky above turns dark
And cold
And the clouds begin to cry.
Does the spark of hope within
Your heart flicker faintly and die?

You're not alone in your loneliness
Others have stood where you stand.
We can help each other see the sun
We can love and live, we can.

It's hard sometime to keep the faith
To believe the sun will ever rise.
It's like spring flowers that push
Through the snow
Life goes on so can you and I.

Together we really can make it
Sharing our strengths along the way.
We may never know the reason why
So let's take life day by day.

You're not alone in your loneliness
Others have stood where you stand
We can help each other see the sun
We can love and live, we can.

Acknowledgements

Thanks to the Apollo Team at CreateSpace for their patience and encouragement in the editing and designing process in the creation of this book.

A special thanks to Michael Leo for technical assistance, to Julie and Pat for their reading and suggestions regarding the manuscript, to Jodi Engebrecht for her thorough proofreading, to Dr. Norman Ellman for his advice, and to Andrew Little and Progressive CDS for their encouragement and cover design.

Limitations
By LauraJo Engebrecht

What must I say to you to know
That you're important to me.
That I await for your arrival
Just to share your company

And when by circumstances
There's no time for us to share
I'm left with such an empty feeling
That life is not fair.

Sunlight warms without a word
Silent rainbows bring us peace
So listen with your heart and
Feel this love that will not cease.

You give to me a gentle touch
And an understanding ear
But you keep your heart protected
I shall never see a tear.

We all have our limitations
We draw the line we will not cross
And we have only ourselves to blame
For all that's won or lost.

Sunlight warms without a word
Silent rainbows bring us peace
So listen with your heart and feel
This love that will not cease
For our love will never cease.

Prologue

Was it all to be? Are we all drawn together by some predestined play written into the Matrix, a divine plan? What was the lesson in the drama of your life—our life together? The courage of your struggle? The helplessness? The anger? The grief? The point, what is the point? If the message is so vague that it is lost in the emotional trauma of its delivery, is it the writer, the director, or the actor who's to blame? Or is blame even an issue?

Where does one begin? Perhaps it is with the birth notice:

"A bouncing baby girl, christened LauraJo, after her grand-parents, born in Lansing Michigan on June 20, 1957 to proud parents, Pat and Ron, weighing 6 lbs 8ozs."

Or do we begin with the death notice:

"LauraJo Engebrecht was laid to rest this first week of January, 1987 at the age of twenty-nine after ten long years of struggle battling a mental illness diagnosed as *Borderline Personality Disorder*. Cause of death: Suicide."

For twenty plus years, your journals have laid in your small, home-made chest, LJ, unread. The whispering started some years ago, but I refused to listen. Instead I built houses, created beautiful gardens, worked with L&L (our family construction firm), or played tennis. I'm sure this doesn't surprise you. We were never a family to address the serious issues that lay between us. But as your voice echoes,

"Here it is, Mom, a few days late...the tape you requested." (Christmas 1983). Reluctantly, I open the family scrapbook tucked into your small, homemade chest, take out Journal #1...now my voice echoes,

"Here it is, LJ, over twenty years late, the book you meant to write."

I have moved the homemade wooden chest into three different homes, locked, journals and poetry unread. Twenty plus years have passed. I pause in my denial. Your whispering grows louder as if you know the sands of time are falling faster through my hourglass.

I enter your writings as logged in your journals, without editing. The teardrops are not transferable, but all else is as you recorded.

It would be simple, almost painless, to believe in predestination— meant to be—but there is something within me that refuses that line of thought: *Too easy*. Somewhere there is a clue. Is it locked away in your chest of journals that I am just beginning to read after all this time? Is there an answer?

Your jousts with death are evident in your sketches, your songs, the pictures taken that first year you were away at college—so many not so subtle hints when looked at from the advantage of time. Like the lyrics, "I can see clearly now, the rain has gone," the rain of emotions, of ego controlling with anger, impatience, pride, inability to communicate—the real flaw in creation.

It's not your time, LJ, I told you. Get on with living! And so you tried.

The following thoughts on death are from Byron Katie, inspirational teacher and creator of *The Work:*

> *"There's no decision in death. People who know that there's no hope are free. The decision is out of their hands. It has always been that way, but some people have to die bodily to find out. No wonder they smile on their deathbeds. Dying is everything they were looking for in life. Their delusion of being in charge is over. When there's no choice, there's no fear. And in that, there is peace. They realize that they're home and that they've never left."*

And you did smile, LJ, a peaceful smile that gave me solace. *Control* seemed to be the issue. You thought the choice of living or dying was yours, and yet time after time your Creator tried to show you that *you* were not in control: That time at the water tower when the grounds keepers only appeared once a month and found you; that time along the highway rest stop when a concerned passerby called the police. Memories of so many other times have faded.

The end? So many things fell into place: the hospital staff releasing you without the proper paperwork from your doctor, the very cold temperatures that fogged your windows giving you a cloud to rest in, protecting you from intrusion, the police patrolling the park turning in a different direction. It was your time to go home.

Chapter One

What kind of family were we? *Ordinary.* Like so many in our era, your father and I married young. He had to get his mother's signature--being only twenty. Men had to be twenty-one to marry in Oregon. I was celebrating my nineteenth birthday and wedding on the same day, December 19, 1954.

Three children in three years! You sandwiched in between your brothers. Your father's grandmother (almost ninety, the mother of nine) took me aside, shook her gnarled finger and said, "You don't have to have a baby every year; they have things these days!" Planned parenthood? I didn't elaborate about failed contraceptives!

Growing Years

Your father, quiet by nature, was busy going to school those early years. I was on overload with all the chores, but I cannot or will not believe that the things your father and I did or did not do propelled you on the journey you took. The indictment by the medical profession regarding the cause of *Borderline Personality Disorder* **(Poor or abusive parenting)** still stands in today's treatment more than twenty years later.

Neither your father nor I had what you might call a *normal* upbringing, but then it seems almost everyone comes from a dysfunctional family. Your father's dad was ill from as far back as he can remember. A late diagnosis of a *brain tumor* explained his seizures, but basically, life on a dairy farm in the forties for your dad didn't include a lot of father-son discussions, or fishing trips in the Cascades, or family vacations. Milking cows twice a day—the life of a dairyman and his family—kept them on the farm.

Your father's dad spent his last years in the state hospital after a massive brain surgery left him unable to function at home. He died when your father was seventeen.

It was Granny who went to see your father play football and basketball in junior high and high school. Granny chose to work in the high school office in order to be a part of his world. Her dedication to Ron was unusual, for parents in those days were not *friends* with their children, they were parents. She sensed that the death of his father left a void, and made an effort to meet his friends and their families—to be involved.

Granny was not possessive of her only son. She welcomed me, reaching out, bringing me into her home, letting me know that I was welcome. Ron and I had her full blessings when we married so young. Laura was a non-interfering mother-in-law. No advice. Even when I announced my third pregnancy in as many years while your father was still going to school, there were only congratulations, even though I'm sure she was questioning our sanity.

Now this may seem trivial, this hands-off relationship between your grandmother and me. It was anything but trivial when you understand that your father was an only child, that Granny had been recently widowed, was running the dairy farm with the help of a hired hand, and that I was a *welfare* child with a very shady background. I'm sure there must have been quiet moments when Granny thought that her only son could have done better. Not once did I ever get that message.

If your father lacked a relationship with his dad, my *mother* training was less than stellar. We (my two sisters and I) were farmed out to anyone that would take us, and if they wouldn't take the three of us, we were separated, always with the promise, "I'll be back!" from our mother.

Secrets and lies and closet shelves--every family has them. Who needed to know all the sordid details? Newspaper headlines, trials: "Mother kicked out of state as *unfit*;" 1946 was oh so long ago. What difference could it possibly make to me? It was all behind me. I was married now, with a *normal* life!

The mother that never was but lived in our imagination. The men, not in our imagination...a parade of faces and hands and burning false teeth. What can children do but accept the life their parents thrust them into? The three of us, Bev, Marion and I, the baby, faced the daily challenges as all children do. In California, when we were living with our cousins, we cut through the sugar beet fields to go to school. The fields were laced with irrigation ditches we had to cross.

"You'd better watch out...quicksand! One slip and you're a goner" My cousin's warnings echoed. My kindergarten legs trembled, preparing me for future broad jumping.

The things you remember--bits and pieces of flotsam and jetsam--the bobby pin in the light socket which set the entire apartment house blowing fuses until it was finally discovered near my bed on the floor.

To this day I do not know what precipitated that strange, middle-of-the night departure with Mother and *him*; three hot, carsick days, the arrival at that tar paper, two-room shack (even at six I knew it was a shack!) that we would call home for the next five years. Where? The middle of nowhere.

And so life settled in—sorta. The three of us together. No more Sally Butts, Aunt Dorees or whomever Mother happened to leave us with--always with that promise echoing, "I'll be right back."

The best thing about the wilderness? *They* were gone almost every day—1941, Portland, Oregon, working in the shipyards, gone from dawn to dusk, leaving us to wander the hills, pick wild flowers, ride the cows and Jerry, our old work horse. Our biggest blessing was Shep, our half collie, half shepherd dog, who slept with us, swam with us, and consoled us with the love and adoration that only a dog can give, filling the void left empty of human love.

We hated the weekends when they were home. We learned to dodge his blows, stay out of harm's way—a cat teasing a leashed dog. My oldest sister, Bev, stuck up for me whenever she could. He seemed to get great pleasure in making life miserable for me like refusing to let me read the funny papers. Bev used to sit at the table and lower the paper down between her knees so I could read them from my crouched position on the floor.

He would bring home oranges, a special treat for *him*. We'd watch him in fascination as he took out his false teeth to gum the orange, but we had the last laugh when he burned up his false teeth with the orange peelings!

Mother never stood up for us. They even took the tube out of the radio (our era's TV) so we couldn't listen and *wear it out* while they were at work. They even tried to take our swimsuits so we couldn't swim in the creek across the road. How dumb was that! Who needed swimsuits?

A terrible childhood? I remember those five years living with my sisters in the foot hills of the Cascades as a child's dream. We were free to explore over a hundred acres of hills, woods shadowing bubbling springs, moss covered stones in lush fern grottos.

Scotch broom filled the pastureland, It's tall broom-like branches reaching skyward as far as we could see. We spent hours losing ourselves from the world wandering through the mazes made by the cattle. The yellow, pea-like blossoms generated pods that matured in late summer. In the still, heavy August air you could hear the song-like snapping of the pods as they ruptured, sending seeds into the air to settle to earth to thicken the already dense growth.

There were cows to milk, pigs to feed, chicken houses to clean, eggs to gather, and Jerry (our old Arabian work horse) to ride when we could entice him over to a stump so we could crawl on him, clutching his mane and each other. It was never a long ride. He always headed straight for the barn and into his stall. The doorway was only inches above his back. Result? As we were scraped off, we would grab at his tail to soften our landing in a pile behind him, laughing and screaming as if surprised by this antic, a most predictable event.

I became a gardener out there in the hills. Each spring the *Rural Box Holder* (that's us) received seed catalogs with brightly colored pictures. Large, bright red tomatoes glistened on the pages next to the shiny green cucumbers and red and white radishes, orange carrots, green beans, lettuce, and so on. There was a fruit section too. Luscious looking strawberries, black berries, apples, and...water melons!

The three of us hung over the pictures salivating, for those were the days of *home grown* fruits and vegetables. If you didn't grow it, you didn't eat it. We experienced government rationing during the war years: sugar, butter, gasoline. Because Mother and he worked in the shipyards, gas was available, but no chewing gum! We chewed the tar that bubbled up from the road on hot summer days.

Each year we dreamed of all the fruits and vegetables pictured in the catalogs. We dug, hoed and watered. Of course, nothing grew. The seedlings barely made it through the rocky soil. The sun beat down. We carried buckets of water from the well for a while and then gave up. But our dreaming never died. Each spring we'd do it all over again, sure that this was going to be *the* year.

We picked strawberries at Mr. Russell's for money and fruit—boxes of the bright red berries always found their way home in our lunch sack. We discovered an abandoned farm set far back from the road. There was an orchard of apple, plum and peach trees, and abandoned berry patches. The rumors of a wild bull kept us on high alert.

Swimming in the creek in the summer was better than any pool ever built. We'd start early before school was out, when the creek ran fresh from the melting snow fields in the lower Cascades. We'd turn blue, feet numb, quivering lips stretched across chattering teeth. We would lie on the road to warm ourselves—on the curve—but kept one ear to the road to listen for approaching logging trucks. We had some narrow escapes--one time Bev fell asleep! You ought to have heard the choice words from that driver's mouth!

In the winter, we'd retreat to the barn where we stacked the bales of hay creating tunnels and forts beneath the haystack. We'd huddle together with treasures and flashlights, talk about neighbors and school kids, but mostly we built the haystack to hide from *him.* Bev never said anything. If it was unspoken, it was as if it didn't happen, especially if you never told anyone.

The scariest time of all for me was when Mother went on some errand and left us alone with *him.* Poor Bev. Me? Well, with Bev's help, I hid on the closet shelf, knees held close to my chest to shrink into the shadows because he was always looking for me to send me out to do some dumb thing like rake the back yard, which was all dirt and stones, while he fooled around with Bev.

I could see him from my high perch, looking down on his bald head as he searched the back of the closet yelling for me to come out. Peed my pants more than once. Of course, Bev was his target. She was sixteen when we were taken away, but it had been going on for years. She never complained. "All in a day's work," she told the judge.

And then he turned to Marion who told the neighbor. I remember that last day at school. I was eleven.

Chapter Two

"Hey, how come the police are taking away your sisters?"

I knew it was a trick. That Jimmy was always trying to get something and he wanted my end of the teeter-totter. "Oh no you don't, Jimmy Holden, I'm not falling for that!" I hooked my legs under the board as Stevie tried to bounce me off.

"No kidding! Look for yourself!" and he pointed over toward the crowd of kids and teachers. I could just see Bev being propelled into the police car.

"Let me down! Let me down!" No more had my feet hit the ground then I jumped off, letting poor old Stevie hit the ground with a shriek. I ran as fast as I could but I was too late; the police car, clouded in dust, turned onto the road and sped away.

"What did they do? What's wrong? Has something happened to Momma?"

I was half crying, half shouting, clawing at Miss Starret's dress. She grabbed my hands and held my frantic scratching away from her.

"Calm down, Patty. I don't know. They just showed us some papers and took your sisters." I pulled away and started to run. "Wait! Wait! Someone..."

That's all I heard as I climbed the fence catching my dress and...

But real life has no haystacks, LJ, as you discovered. What tales did I tell you that so disturbed you? The bad stuff lies buried, rarely thought of, and never spoken. What good is remembering, rehashing old nightmares? What did all that have to do with you? I could go on and tell you about having to give away Shep, being separated from my sisters, being put into a foster *cover* home that summer with the Eskelsons, who *kept* kids to work their farm—pick berries, milk cows—until a permanent foster home could be found.

And it was. Mr. and Mrs. Hodges. They lived in a big white house with a front porch with big round pillars. It looked like Tara to me (Gone with the Wind). A beautiful weeping birch, rich, green lawn all surrounded with a meticulously clipped laurel hedge. They were rich! Had to be. He owned a meat market, locker plant, grocery store—a strip mall in today's setting. Why would they want to take in a stray, welfare kid?

Mother? She took his side in the trial even though she knew what was happening. He went to jail and she had to leave the state. It was all there in the newspaper for all the world to see.

I mourned the loss of a mother that never was. Mrs. Hodges successfully separated me from Marion and Bev and I grew up hating all that was or had been.

My drive was fired with anger, a friend not a foe, for it drove me to excel, *to show them.* I was never sure who *them* was: Mrs. Hodges, my foster mother; Mrs. Wesson, my caseworker; the teachers at school; the kids?

Did I *belong?* I never asked that question. It was never an issue. My need was not to be *as good as* but to be *better than.* Time has allowed me to see that the *them* I was trying to show was *me.*

I gave up on the idea of ever having a home with a mother and a father like other kids. What was a father good for anyway? Didn't see much good that men did for Mother. So my life was different…It was all something that I had learned to live with, forgetting the *yuck* and concentrating on the fun times, and there are always *fun times.*

When I regaled you with stories of the young bull chasing me through the field, hunting down the cows when they escaped, swimming in the creek, you must have been zeroing in on the *haystack* we built to escape. Your brothers, or your nieces and nephews pay little attention to the books I have written, the stories I tell, but, with time, I see that you were so much more sensitive. You seemed to see through the laughter to the hidden, secret places! Was your devotion an attempt to make it up to me?

Chapter Three

Going To School

It seemed everyone was going to school in the fifties except me, of course. We were married during Christmas vacation of your father's junior year in college. I worked at the college that first year while your father went to class during the days and worked in the lab, often past midnight, on his experiments to earn his PhD.

Your father was really concerned about my education...suggested that I take some courses on television, a new opportunity for our era. How did he ever talk me into chemistry? By assuring me he'd help. The course was scheduled at 7 AM! Guess where he was. And so you children became my educators.

Summer school in Lansing, Michigan: A National Science Foundation grant for your father (the Sputnik era) sent us off to Michigan State University in June 1957. You made your appearance on this earth two days after we arrived, June 20.

It was a quick delivery, nothing unusual to start your life, no thunder and lightning, no hint of any pending disaster.

The trip back to Oregon six weeks later was hot, humid, with no air-conditioned car. You cried. And cried! We (you and I) stayed in the car while your father and brother, Jeff, slept in the motel. You cried. Finally, after checking for pins, feeding, and so on, I did the unthinkable for a mother—I left you for an hour to catch some sleep. Was that when it started? When you were left unguarded, did some dark entity enter your psyche? Did you feel abandoned? Was it then that a seed of darkness, an emptiness wrapped your heart and grew allowing no light of love to enter?

Mothers

We all have a mother and most women succumb to being one. Famous? Who comes to mind but Mother Teresa, the mother of the world, and the Queen Mother, very busy running a country. Stay-at-home moms are rare these days, but not so for us. For a short time I worked, then Granny helped us financially through the *school* days which lasted years. You were all going to grow up and go to school like Dad. His home was the lab until he took the job at Kodak and we moved to Rochester when you were seven.

What is it that makes a good mother? Has anyone who has had children ever come through the experience without asking themselves that question? We all know the biology part, the heredity part, and today we are aware of the "smoking, drinking, diet, and exercise," the physical part.

There are mothers who hover, solicit, and stroke; they are called, *Smother Mothers*. Single mothers who work day and night to feed, clothe, and educate their children; are called *Absentee Mothers*. Mothers who are ambitious in their careers are called *Selfish Mothers* and on and on. And so we try.

Michael Singer's comparing *mother* love to God's love in *The Untethered Soul* irritates me. The perfect love? It is an absurd notion that biologically having a child automatically leads to the perfect mother love! Some mothers hold their newborn child and are overwhelmed by the miracle of life (I counted fingers and toes). There are the sacrificing mothers who would give their life and sometimes do for their children, who seem to be incomplete, whose very existence is their children—an intensity of love that I lacked. Was I deficient? Did I miss a gene? Was it selfish of me to want something from life besides the *mothering* part?

There was so much to do with the cooking, cleaning, yard chores. I was always there watching, scolding, applauding all of you in your efforts, reading bedtime stories, dusting you off when you got sand in your eyes…all this, is that not love? Looking back now, I pause with a feeling of regret as I realize how few quiet moments I took to hold and nurture any of you. I guess I just didn't know how.

Your doctor asked me how I felt when I was pregnant with you. My flippant reply of "fat!" wasn't the whole story. Jeff was only six months old when I became pregnant with you. This *motherhood* was a new thing—your father in graduate school, I had not lost the thirty pounds I had gained with Jeff, and I was used to being thin. I did not want to be pregnant again. Birth control was less than perfect in those days and so you learned to accept the backache, the stretch marks from the rapid weight gain, the sleepless nights, and (after you were born) the crying. You were a crier.

Three babies crying, demanding feeding, changing. The small clipping sent to me by Granny was magnetized to the refrigerator: *Before I had children, I had three ideas about raising them. Now I have three children and no ideas.* Who had time to read Dr. Spock? Besides, what did he know? He was a man!

I ask again, how does one learn to be a mother? Sorry, I was too busy to give it a whole lot of thought. Did I worry about your psyche? No! It was feed the babies, change the babies, shop, cook, and clean. Perhaps it was the potty training. Could I have wounded your psyche over that? We didn't have disposable diapers... "Is there a diaper in the toilet?" was the echoing cry from your father. So much talk amongst my friends was about potty training...an early goal to be accomplished.

You and I had a go around about that. You talked at sixteen months and I expected you to tell me when you had to go. The pressure became evident when nap time became your time of relief. I realized the pressure I was placing on you and ceased my efforts. Today, doctors warn of the psychological stress the child feels and advise parents not to make it an issue. Children are three and four before they graduate from Pampers.

Today's mothers combine raising children with their workaday schedules. They too read *how-to* manuals and magazines, watch television talk shows, and, of course, listen with resignation to their parents' unwanted advice. What is the latest edict? Who is today's Dr. Spock? Mothers continue to ask, "Are we doing it right?" We seek approval from our friends, our doctors, and admit it, now and then from our parents trying to forget their threat, "I hope someday you have a child just like you!"

As mothers, we're all beginners doing the best we can, only to hear our grown-up children issuing their complaints: "You never...I..." while dutifully sending the insipient, sticky sweet cards on Mother's Day, cards that rhyme declaring the perfection of love, patience, long suffering, sacrifice.

Forget the shouted, "I hate you!" The stamping of small feet growing into sullen looks; the slamming doors that eventually grow into, "Mom's coming! I have to clean the cupboards, straighten the closets, bite my lip and ignore the knot in my gut when she tells me that the children are drinking too much soda, eating too much junk, texting, have earphones glued, and not picking up their clothes."

I read your journals to learn of your thoughts. I am tolerated by your brothers with quiet resignation when I (and I try not to) offer my *outdated advice.* Your words on parenting echo, "Mother, haven't you learned that you're damned if you do and damned if you don't?" Those words after you interrupted me quarreling with Jeff over a deed left undone. You grabbed us, turned us back to back, "Now take ten steps, turn, and shoot!"

Miscommunications lie between the generations like deep chasms eroded by so much emotions and unspoken words. So many parents are alienated from their children over the *I-thoughtthat-you-thought* that goes to our graves with us.

"I didn't say that!" (My denial when Jeff accused me of critical words.)

"No, but that's what you meant!"

If I were honest, I'd admit that he was right a good share of the time. Children are so perceptive; communication so flawed.

Parenting Skills

Dr. Spock's book on raising children lay unopened on the back shelf. Your father and I had a crash course with the three of you. Communication skills? "We had three kids before I knew Ron didn't like kids!" I laughingly explained.

It was a joke, of course, but a clue about how much we talked to each other. But what do you know when you're nineteen and twenty? Does age make a difference? Your brothers married much later, each counseled by the marrying priest and minister laying a hint of groundwork for their unions. Ours was all trial and error, as, in my opinion, most marriages truly are.

Overwhelmed? Not much time to think. We had no help from nearby, doting grandparents, no money for baby sitters. We rolled up our sleeves and did what had to be done.

I look at those early pictures of you, LJ, corn silk hair–so curly–large saucer, green/brown eyes. We called you our Campbell Soup girl. You were chubby—took you forever to walk. Jeff got down and crawled with you and Kurt was already on the scene before you took those first steps.

LJ (14 months) Baldwin's Crossing, Sedona, Arizona, summer 1958

Student Family Life

You did not know your father those first years. Thanks to your grandmother's financial assistance, I was a stay-at-home mom. Fourteen months after you were born, your brother, Kurt, arrived.

While your father was at school, my days were spent cleaning the house (we were one of the lucky ones that owned a small house in Corvallis, Oregon), changing diapers, washing diapers, folding diapers (three babies soiling diapers, the kind you had to wash), managing the household, mowing the lawn, and planting the gardens. I always smiled when people asked me if I *worked*! But…"I don't do garages!" I informed your father. He just nodded sagely since we didn't have a garage, just a carport.

A real family at last! Just like everyone else. Unlike me, you didn't have to wonder if I'd be gone in the morning, like my mother. Your room was decorated with lilac print, your brothers' with brightly colored chenille spreads. Life was steady, and predictable.

Your father was off to the lab every day in those early years; his presence edged your days only briefly. And then we moved to New York and he had a regular job (chemist at Kodak) and we had our home—a three bedroom, one and a half bath mansion with a big yard bordered by a small creek perfect for damming and catching minnows. *"I never thought they'd live to grow up!"* (Granny's words after you were grown.)

I guess it was a little dangerous to let you come careening down the hill (public road), all three of you in the wagon, yelling and screaming as you roared across our yard and into the creek. Looked like fun to me!

Fear? What could you possibly have to fear? It wasn't until Kurt was fully grown that I learned he was afraid of the big kitten rug with the Cheshire grin that Granny had braided for him. Every morning I would find it rumpled under his bed and, unthinking, I would drag it out and straighten it.

I guess *unthinking* is the key word here, for what child doesn't have their fears? What child doesn't want to be their parents' favorite, or want to be pretty, smart, liked by their peers. Everyone wants to be popular. When should we have taken your anger, LJ, at not being accepted seriously? How dull witted could we have been?

I look back and blanch at my casual approach to your needs and activities. That time, LJ, when I sent you off to New York to a tennis tournament. Put you on the plane by yourself and it wasn't until you called that I realized I had not sent you with the proper information. The telephone call still echoes, your tears, sobbing into the phone that you were lost and there was no one there to meet you. I panicked, of course but you took control, as in the flood years later, knocked on a stranger's door and they took you to the courts. You must have been fourteen. What kind of mother would do that? *I never thought they'd live to grow up!* echoes.

Perhaps if you'd had a mother like Sue, Kurt's wife, who gets down on the ground and hugs her children and tells them she loves them when they are going to the playground next door, or maybe my friend, Bettye Sue, who is a warm fuzzy. Everyone loves Betty Sue who is the first at everyone's door when trouble knocks.

Neither your father nor I are *touchy-feely* people. Where would we have learned to be, or can it be learned? Was that what you needed? We tucked you in bed, read bedtime stories, listened to your prayers and, *"Leave the door open, please, Mommy."* was just fine with me.

Both your father and I had grown up in an era where there was a distinct division between parent and child. Parents were parents not friends. Our own parental supervision was the *watchful* kind allowing you your failures. If you fell, we didn't run to pick you up but watched to see how you handled the situation. Your childhood injuries were tested: "Are you blooding?" A teasing question we engaged to lessen the fear.

Even the serious accidents: Kurt, when he was five was hit with a softball hit by his brother, Jeff—in the groin—I thought. I packed it with ice. He was calm when I left for a meeting with friends. The call several hours later from your dad brought me home. Kurt cried fitfully throughout the night. We called the doctor in the early morning hours, a rushed trip to the hospital. Emergency surgery for a perforated lower bowel, an acute case of peritonitis. Even after the diagnosis, the seriousness of it all did not register. *I never thought they'd live to grow up*!

With all the family's sporting activities—skiing, tennis, basketball, football, soccer—we experienced few accidents, no broken bones. Kurt was carried off regularly from the soccer fields with twisted ankles, knees, but nothing requiring hospitalization. We had no family doctor—no need. There were no TV ads for medicine, or lawyer ads for injuries. Good *common sense* was the byword. Children were not thought of as *fragile* or was it just us?

Communication

We adopted the framework that we were raised in (parents were boss!) and did not negotiate. Ours was not a *democratic* household. The rules were established and we expected you to abide by them. You all made it easy. There was no rebellion. We had fun together, laughter around the dinner table. We went to your school events: athletics, concerts, PTA, teacher conferences. We sent cookies or cupcakes when it was your turn. Was it *"Life with Father?"* (A popular TV program showing the mother, a fancy apron covering her pretty dress, serving the dinner on a table set with napkins and tablecloth. The father was always fair in his teaching—never impatient or angry.) Well, maybe not so perfect, but what family is?

Did we talk out the serious things? Anger? Hurt feelings? I watch your brothers raise their children and see them building communication bridges. They are aware of those moments when *feelings* need to be expressed, and invite their children to speak their piece.

Our communications skills were minimal at best. I shake my head in wonder at how insensitive your father and I were over the *cataclysmic* events in your lives: If you weren't invited to a birthday party or asked to dance; If you didn't win recognition for a scholastic endeavor. We uttered our words of condolences and expected you to *get on with it…life.*

We forget. As we mature, these events seem insignificant; we forget how we felt, how important it was to us at the time. No one ever took our feelings seriously or even talked to us about these things. To this day, neither your father nor I ever discuss *feelings.* As a family, we have not talked of your death, each of us searching our own psyches, wondering where to put the blame we carry regarding our part in your drama, our insensitiveness that could possibly have been the seed to your destruction.

We now realize that this communication doesn't start with the big events: the washing away of our home with the break in the Barge Canal, the crashing of the car when Jeff and Kurt were driving to college, or your first suicide attempt. It starts when you aren't invited to Suzie's birthday party, when no one invites you to sit with them at lunch, or dance with you, and you deny and stuff the hurt feelings or reach out and retaliate with anger, or in the more accepted ways of competition on tennis courts and basketball courts. Being a winner in these events proved to be a hollow victory for you.

Jodi, your brother Jeff's wife, was much more cognizant of the dangers of un-acceptance. When Julie, their oldest daughter, moved into high school and was teetering on insecurity with her peers, Jodi arranged with the office to have her lunch period coincide with Kyle's, her more gregarious older brother. This helped Julie move into high school with more confidence.

You had such bravado, LJ. Why couldn't I see through it to the suffering? It was only later that I learned that in high school you never went to lunch—no one to sit with. That Ms. Danaher, your gym teacher, left the equipment door unlocked so that you could retrieve a basketball to shoot baskets at noon.

And so you grew. All three of you were good students, fine athletes, responsible. Did we take your talents for granted? It is only now that I realize how very seldom we actually told you how proud we were of you. I guess both your father and I thought that *showing up* and applauding at all of your endeavors was testimony to our feelings of love and support.

Chapter Four

An Ideal Life

Is there such a thing? You played and fought with your brothers, all so close in age. You always held your own at whatever game— the Tarzan swing across the creek where you always made it to the other side, but Jeff often fell off halfway landing in the creek.

LauraJo, age 9, Brook Hollow

I have a small framed picture of
Me when I was a child.
I'm swinging from the Tarzan rope
Wearing an impish smile.

There is something about those eyes
So big and dark, cheerful and round
That calls to me in echoed cries
With a love that knows no bounds.

Come play with me like we used to
I'm no dragon to put away!
I'm more real than your own reflection
And I'll not slip into a cave.

Please don't blame in embarrassment
Your childish acts on me.
Tho I may be the child in you
You're the fruit of the seed.

A little voice so far away
Asking for love returned…
And now I know I need her too
At last I've finally learned.
LJE

We kept waiting for all of you to outgrow us, to prefer your friends, but you didn't. Maybe we should have questioned this friend business a little closer. The three of you played together or with us on family outings. I remember one time when a small boy came over to play with Jeff when he was about ten. I overheard your brothers,

"How long do you think he'll stay?" Kurt asked.

"I don't know, but maybe if we ignore him, he'll go home."

There were no kid birthday parties like your brothers' children enjoy—mostly family gatherings. I didn't think much about it since neither your father nor I ever had parties growing up. His was *family-life* vacations on the beach, at the cabin in the mountains, holidays. Our family life was patterned after his with all of us sharing tennis, vacation adventures to the mountains for skiing, the beach for sand and sun, camping—your sticks poking fires.

Camping, Adirondacks

Family vacation, Martha's Vineyard, 1975

In spite of all the things we did together as a family, for you it never seemed enough. You needed—no—demanded more attention than I was capable of giving. With impatience, I would brush you off, "Go out and play, LJ...not now, maybe later...no, I can't read to you, I'm busy!"

As you grew, my responses continued, "I can't go raspberry picking right now, LJ; take the dog for a walk, would you? Hit some (tennis balls)? We'll just get mad at each other; why don't you practice on the bang board, or call Patty."

My responses silenced your requests. You learned to play by yourself.

Would it have made a difference if I had become your playmate? What was the matter with me? Always busy, three babies in as many years, your father always away at the lab those first years. Excuses? I search for clues.

Chapter Five

You and I will never know how we would be as two grown women—you as a mother, me as a grandmother. Granny was a great mother-in-law, hard to live up to her silences. I've told your brothers' wives not to worry; there was only one woman who truly loved her mother-in-law. It was in the Book of Ruth in the Bible: "Whither thou goest"

But in many ways, you made every day *Mother's Day* for me. Does that sound trite? How was I to know that so much of your attention to me was a symptom of a deep, disturbing need? At times, I sensed it and felt--not exactly anger--but inadequate because I knew I was not and could not be the *everything* you seemed to need, that my fractured, imperfect love for you was not enough.

The *doing* of life oftentimes leaves little time for the *being.* I must admit my love for you was not always evident. It tugged at me in snatches of momentary adoration…the sight of your tousled curly hair on the pillow just before you fell asleep, the satisfaction of your arrival at your destination still decently attired, hair almost combed, socks matching, of watching you and Jeff reach out and stand in front of Kurt, protecting your little brother.

As the years pass, I begin to understand that life is *trivia,* the little things and now I see that there were many moments when I was too busy, too distracted to notice your need, but why were you so needy?

Misfit

It became very evident quite early in your school years that you were not popular, that you were a thwarted leader, not able to follow, but without the charisma or willingness to develop leadership skills.

Rebel? Not exactly in the true sense of the word—more of a loner, always pushing the *authority* figure for control. Your talent set you apart: athletically, musically, artistically. The awards poured in and we complacently felt that your self-esteem was intact. How could you not feel good about yourself? Look at the trophies, the blue ribbons.

Playing by the rules

You never could, LJ, even as a little kid, five, six years old. Your brothers and other children would be playing in the yard. You'd arrive on the scene and within ten minutes the game would fall apart because you changed the rules and they wouldn't play by yours, and you couldn't seem to play by theirs.

Was that the beginning of your death wish? The first step? How could we have changed that? Your struggles with the teachers, a repeated pattern. Every year the battles began, the ground rules set–the conferences.

With some teachers, you called a truce and reluctantly worked within *their rules*. Some even became your mentors, while others remained your adversaries. Remember the English teacher whose favorite author was Herman Melville? You hated Moby Dick. "Too wordy, Mom." Little wonder that when you started your essay with, "Was Melville paid by the word?" You ended up with an *F*.

"You want me to get an *A*, Mom?"

You proceeded to *brown-nose* your way through the next paper on still another Melville story and received an *A*. You were always putting people's *feet to the fire*, so to speak: coaches, peers, doctors, and friends, even me. When one of your brothers was breaking a rule, you would announce it to me quite loudly and stand, hands on hips, waiting for me to enforce it-- whether I felt like it or not. That day I didn't care if Jeff played in the water, but I had told him not to the day before. So who was I mad at? *You,* of course, for forcing the issue. You inherited my need to *be right.* Obnoxiously *right!* I have plaques from my friends: Rule #1: Pat is always right. Rule #2: When Pat is wrong, refer to Rule #1.

Unpopular? Yes, but not self destructive because of it. Like you, I excelled in sports. I received my satisfaction by being the only girl on the boy's tumbling team and being the boys' first choice when choosing teams. I expected you to get the same satisfaction by being on the boy's tennis team.

You seemed immune to kids' taunts. If they made fun of your clothes, you'd wear them for a week. When you grew old enough to go to school dances, you'd go alone and ask the boys to dance, or dance alone. I could not even imagine such courage. In our time, the girls would sit together or cry in the bathroom because nobody asked them to dance. You never waited. I remember you telling me nonchalantly about one of the boy's response to your invitation,

"With you, you dog!"

I harbor hatred for that unknown boy, then and now, who added one more stone to your inner wall. We all remember words we wished we had not spoken. He, too, will remember.

Anger

How did we handle anger in the family? "Go to your room until you can apologize," was our standard response.

You couldn't understand why Kurt didn't applaud your attack on the boy that was hitting him, an action that got you suspended from the bus. Kurt's response? He was embarrassed when the kids taunted him, "Is your sister here to protect you?"

And so you stuffed, and hit. Remember the *No-Hit chart?* You were in the third or fourth grade when hitting became a problem. We consulted with the teacher and came up with the chart awarding you stars plus other small rewards when you went days without hitting.

Friends

As a family we enjoyed sports together: tennis, skiing, camping. There was always someone to play with. Team sports at school also provided interaction for all of you, but there wasn't the one-on-one special friend for any of you. I remember sending Jeff off to camp when he was about twelve, a privilege, we thought. His loud exclamation upon his return?

"If you ever do that again, I'm going to divorce you!"

Peers

Neither your brothers nor you were heavily peer oriented, which made it easy for us. You played with each other. *Friends?* You might say we were all *friends*; we worked and played together. When Jeff went off to college, the first separation from the family circle, we told him he could not take Kurt with him.

You didn't seem to need friends, or so we thought. A friend? Of course you needed a friend; everyone needs a friend. I was your mother not your friend, but it went deeper than you wanting me to be your playmate. You had me on a pedestal. Your devotion made me uncomfortable. If anyone knew I didn't belong on a pedestal, it was me. I couldn't be the person you wanted, needed me to be. Guilt wrapped me when you were more grown up than I was in forgiving and apologizing. What I didn't understand was that the intensity of your love for me was a symptom of a deep seeded need. Perhaps you sensed my own need for love. Most of us love with Ego love, wanting something in return; our love is portioned out conditionally. Over the years, I have mistaken the intensity of your love for me as *Unconditional love,* but I was wrong. *Unconditional love* has no need.

It was not that I didn't think it a bit unusual that you would make my bed, help clean up after parties, fold up the clothes without my asking. My friends were envious of your *thoughtfulness.* Should I have questioned this? Unusual? Perhaps, but sick?

Money

Your moneymaking endeavors: mowing lawns, shoveling snow, stringing rackets, and so on, all came about when your father and I made a decision after overhearing a telephone conversation between Jeff and the neighbor. That conversation?

"No, I guess not." Jeff hung up the phone.

"What was that all about, Jeff?"

"Oh, Mr. Piazza wanted me to mow his lawn, but I didn't feel like it."

After a powwow with your Dad, we announced at the dinner table: "No more sporting equipment." If you wanted a tennis racket, new skis, or a bike, you had to earn the money and pay for it yourself. The three of you became entrepreneurs. Results? You had the best sporting equipment in the neighborhood and took very good care of it.

Allowances? You all were expected to do chores around the house—make your beds, clean your rooms, do the dishes, mow the lawn. We passed on our own youthful lessons that you didn't get to play until your work was done. If you were invited to birthday parties, you had to buy the present with your own money. (*They're not my friends,* I explained.) I remember Jeff's words when I asked him why he wasn't going to a birthday party, "I don't like him that much!" And when you grew old enough to date, we did not pay.

I remember Kurt's comment to me when I was aghast at the cost of taking a girl to the prom: flowers, dinner, limo… I told him *that his father had never spent that much money on a date with me. "Well, Mom, we date classy girls!"*

Athletic

I remember your father throwing balls for the boys to bat, and you too, of course. Swing and miss, swing and miss, swing and, "Maybe she can take dancing lessons!" Your father shook his head. Little did we know that you would outperform your brothers on the athletic fields. The trophies that washed away in the flood were there for basketball and tennis. When you were a freshman and wanted to try out for the boys tennis team (1972 New York State Law Chapter IX allowed girls to try out for the boys teams in non-contact sports), the coach refused.

"Try out for the JVs, LJ," the coach told you, and then invited Kurt to be on the team.

"But I can beat Kurt," you told him, "let me challenge."

It was the JVs or nothing you were informed, so off you went to the athletic director. "You've hired a male chauvinist for a tennis coach, Sir!" You exited that meeting much calmer than he; and you started on the boys' varsity team that very next year—with a different tennis coach.

Chapter Six

Tennis

It was your senior year, that last match: Pittsford against Brighton to win the Sectionals for a chance to compete in the state tournament. You were down 2-5, third set to Ronnie Pinsky for the championship team point. Drop shot…you ran, fell, scrambled up, retrieved your racket, and somehow got the ball back, ran for the lob, and won that point! Did you not hear the applause and shouts of your teammates as they watched Ronnie blow his cool? He never won another game. Thanks to your win, Pittsford-Sutherland went to the state tournament.

How can we ever forget your exhibition match at the War Memorial in Rochester when you and Billy Nealon played Bobby Riggs and Jimmy Arias? How could that not have been *the* night to remember? Riggs had just been defeated by Billy Jean King (your idol) in the *War of the Sexes* on national television and here you were on the court with the famous *jester.*

1972 Rochester War Memorial; Exhibition Match between LauraJo Engebrecht and Billy Nealon vs. Bobby Riggs and Jimmy Arias from Buffalo

Etched on your trophies were many titles: New York State Doubles Champion in the eighteen-and-under when you were sixteen, Tennis Club of Rochester Club Champion, a walk-on in tennis at the University of Arizona where you played #1 on the woman's tennis team with a full scholarship for the brief time you were there.

You loved this picture, LJ: "Look at my muscles, Ma."

Laura Jo Engebrecht (left) breezed to women's singles crown

Tennis was your life in those teenage years. You and your brothers spent your summer on the courts, competing in tournaments. I remember your trip to St. Louis the summer of your seventeenth birthday: you, Kurt, Jeff, Kevin, and Pierre. Were we crazy to let the five of you travel across country—one of your first journeys without adult supervision? Jeff was nineteen and very dependable.

Winning or losing on the tennis courts turned out not to be the lesson. When you flew home to play in another tournament, I remember your entry into the house—door slamming, your voice loud with indignation, "Boys are Gross!" We didn't ask. It was only later in your struggle to overcome did you share with us the letter from Kevin who was studying to be a priest:

> *Remember, LJ, how we spent the whole trip to St. Louis trying to gross you out...how we jumped off the balcony into the pool, how we told the motel owner there were only three of us...how we tried to convince Pierre that he truly needed deodorant by lining up and applying it to ourselves and handing it to him who promptly threw it away saying, "You, Americans...too clean!"*

We never knew all the details, as most parents don't—our salvation—but I believe that your image of boys dropped a notch or two on that trip.

It seemed you were on the sports page often with your tennis/basketball victories, but then there were failures too, the disappointment when you were eighteen. I remember how excited you were to get an invitation to play in the Nationals. You were back on the courts practicing and then the rejection in the mail. You didn't qualify—not enough tournaments. By this time, the dark cloud had already begun to settle over you.

Chapter Seven

Basketball #15

Along with your tennis you wore the light blue jersey, #15, a number you wore for four years playing basketball on PittsfordSutherland's championship team.

Was I remiss when I allowed you, when faced with an ultimatum by the coach, to make the decision to quit the basketball team your senior year? In hindsight so many lessons seem clear. You were so determined. Did we discuss your position, your obligation to the team? No. I knew you were the touchstone for the team, having played with them for four years. In some ways, you were their coach *on the floor*. When your coach demanded you apologize to the referee, backed you into a corner in front of your team mates and gave you an ultimatum to comply with her demands or you were off the team, your position was rock solid— freedom of speech. You pointed out that you didn't swear at the referee, but had just told her she had *won* another one for the opposing team because of her *unfair* calls—all this in the heat of competition.

Your team never won another game. Who did they blame? You, of course; you became an outcast where you had been the central spirit inspiring them to do their best. Did I foresee this? Should I have gone with you to the coach? By this time, you were seventeen and had become your own decision maker. You were adamant that you had the right to voice your own opinion. In your mind, it was your coach who had drawn the line in the sand. Of course, you did not back down. Today, I read of a young girl being defended by the ACLU for her right to *freedom of speech* when her school suspended her for three days for voicing her opinion on *Facebook* regarding the quality of a teacher. And the world turns.

The ribbons on the wall were not only for athletics. There was the blue ribbon for the oak desk you created for me: "To write your Pulitzer prize on, Ma."

That was another battle won. When you signed up for shop your sophomore year in high school, you were told, *girls* didn't take *shop*, they take *Home Ec.* (1972).

"But I don't want to take *Home Ec.*, I want to take *shop!*" And the crusade began. Every day you baked cookies or cakes and took them in to the principal.

"See, I already know how to cook, I want to take *shop!*" To no avail. *Home Ec.* it was.

"Well, it wasn't a complete waste, Ma, now I know the name of the lettuce I like: *Iceberg!*"

By your senior year, girls were allowed to take shop. How much did your crusade open the door?

Chapter Eight

How quickly life changes. Such a beautiful October day, the twenty-ninth, 1974. You had just come home from school. I sat barefoot on the family room floor sorting the mail when he hit the front door banging and shouting,

"Get the hell out, it's coming! Get in your car and go!" By the time I'd opened the door, he was half way to the neighbor's house. "Go!" he yelled over his shoulder. I had no clue, but whatever *it* was left little doubt that we were in danger. I looked around.

"Where's my purse?" Everything seemed in slow motion.

"Here, Ma." You were taking your car keys apart and handing me the ones to the station wagon.

Did I hear it first or see the wall of water churning, not an alarming roar, but a more sinister, almost silent sluicing down the ravine. I backed the car up the road to the top of the hill, got out, and looked back. You were in the Pinto—the one that wouldn't start unless you fastened your seat belt, which always stuck. I could see you yanking at it.

"Get out and run!" I yelled. By this time, the wave was breaking out of the ravine across the road. You finally got the car started—too late to use the road, so you backed through Delaney's yard and up the road to join me. We stood silently watching as the house shuddered against the impact, hold for a moment, and then break from its foundation and float like a houseboat until it crashed and splintered into McCurdy's house, the roof and pieces carried away by the torrent.

My mind was blank. I stood outside myself watching. I heard a whine and looked down at Fred, our dog who was nudging me, licking my hand. You had saved him.

Engebrecht house fragments, October 29, 1974

If I had not been so myopic in my own disorientation, I would have seen you floundering, searching not only the woods for the pieces of your life, but seeking the "Home" that you thought existed at #1 Brook Hollow. Of course you could not know that "Home" was not the trophies lost, the movies we watched at Christmas time…you the leading role announcing the calendar year–starting–how many years back? It was a tradition…watching you children grow before our eyes. Now it is gone, this movie record of our celebrations…indeed a Kodak moment.

You hugged your treasures close, a clarinet filled with mud, a bent tennis trophy, an unopened can of tennis balls. You were triumphant in discovering our bedroom chest with your father's amethyst/diamond tie clasp still in the top drawer. It was the kitchen stove with a roast still in the oven that reminded you of scenes from the "Last Days of Pompeii" With each discovery your grip on reality fell into the shadow land.

The way it was: LJ's sketch of our home at #1 Brook Hollow

Flood insurance? Nobody on the street had flood insurance, or in the entire town for that matter. Our home owner's insurance? Those famous words: *You're not covered.* Flood? Act of God? I always find it interesting that we blame such natural calamities on God. But this wasn't a *natural* disaster—the lawyers lined up.

We moved in with Granny and began to rebuild, but where do you begin when everything is gone?

You and I (neither of the boys were home--Jeff, off to college, Kurt at soccer practice, your father at work) witnessed it all. Did you have nightmares? Of course, why wouldn't you? Me? I was numb. Friends and strangers poured to our rescue.

"You have to let me help you," came the voice of a stranger over the phone. And she came with a lovely set of china to start over. I learned to *receive*. I had always kept a mental ledger, never wanting to be *beholden, always* kept even with gifts, invitations, favors. So many friends and strangers came to our aid. I began to understand Shakespeare's, *quality of mercy is twice blessed, him that gives and him that receives.*

That was the year your father and I learned to drink coffee. The Red Cross wagon was parked on our street for weeks as twenty-five families tried to put their lives back together. Of those families, there were many divorces—adversity pulling them apart.

We were the lucky ones; there was nothing to salvage, no mud to shovel out of the basement, no walls to pull apart, no shoes to wear, except for Annemarie's, a friend in need, indeed. A pair of shoes with a history—the same pair that went back to her when her house burned five years later.

Was it because I'd been shuttled around my entire young life from aunt to stranger to foster home that I knew that home was in your heart and that we'd rebuild? How could you have known? It never occurred to me to get counseling for you. It wasn't done in those days—counseling children who have experienced tragedies. Did we talk? I was too busy with the *doing* of rebuilding to notice that you were floundering, that it wasn't just a house that had washed away; it was your world.

Your classmates gathered around. All your trophies were gone, washed away in the canal waters. The same classmates who had shunned you over the years now tried to reach out to you. They researched and created a plaque with many of the titles and presented their gift to you at graduation.

The Coming of Age

Where is the child
Who by the sea
Was swept away
With beauty,
I measurably captured
In tiny hands
Held only as time
Holds the wind swept sands.
Like clockwork
The ebbing tide
Shrinks the wide eyes,
Causing countless
Treasures to fall
By the wayside.
Grey as the dawn
On a misty morn,
Alone and naked
The truth is born.

Chapter Nine

And so you graduated. We celebrated life and your many accomplishments.

Granny LJ Ron Pat

Graduating in the top ten percent of your class was no surprise to us, for you excelled in everything you undertook. For graduation, you and I went off to Hawaii. Your brothers had chosen to go with Ron on a ski trip. It was on that trip that I became aware of your beginning melancholy. On the way home, we stopped at the University of Arizona in Tucson. You met the coach and hit some tennis balls with some other girls, an effort that resulted in the offer of a full tennis scholarship. You played number one the season you were there.

The summer between graduation and your leaving for college was one of building our new home on Lodge Pole, high above the canal. You chose to wait until winter term to leave for college. You needed a place to call *home,* and the house was not completed yet. We carried railroad ties, laid brick, planted tees, terraced the hillside. It was a summer of healing for us, but you? We moved in November. Home! Or was it?

Our new home on Lodgepole

The tie wall and brick patio you helped build.

After the holidays, you flew off to Arizona to meet your first big challenge away from home. Should I have flown west with you? By this time, you were experienced in flying to tennis tournaments, meeting people. You seemed so nonchalant about it all or was it I who was nonchalant?

***A note I found tucked in a book—no date—about your departure to college.

The years we've shared have formed my life
Into what it is. The fun, the strife
All the love and all the tears.
We've shared them through my growing years.
You've made me whole, you're a part of me
But now I go to try to be
A person, an individual, maybe a bit loud
At times, but one of whom I hope you're proud!
You and me, seems a bit strange
Almost as though
It were prearranged that we should be so close,
So much a friend, mother, companion, life's teaching pro.
I leave you now, not saying goodbye
Only take care of yourself, and I
Shall be back before your winter's fire
Burns low, filled with adventure, filled with desire.
Look to the future
I am there.
All my love,
Your daughter, LauraJo

PS…The doll is for your desk. It is you and me. It reminded me of all those times I needed a little extra love and understanding. You were always there and I thank you. Take care now. Xxxx

Chapter Ten

University of Arizona

I can see now what I didn't see then—a smile hiding the tears.

At the U of A you were rushed by several sororities. It was all so very exciting and normal for most young girls, but almost overwhelming to you—to be wanted. Why wouldn't they want you? Tennis star, good student, cute, but you saw something different looking back from that mirror.

Acceptance came too late. All those years of rejection built such a solid wall, a boundary not allowing you to believe that anyone could want you. The rush from the sororities inviting you to become one with them was unbelievable for you. Playing number one on the tennis team did not convince you. Ekhart Tolle speaks of the *Pain Body* in *The New Earth* and *Power of Now*. Had your *Pain Body* become such a part of you, your boundaries fortified by your many rejections, convincing you that you were "unlovable"? Had all that become part of your self-identity? In Deepak Chopra's book, *Reinventing the Body, Resurrecting the Soul*, it is written:

"It's one thing to feel unloved, but for some, I am unlovable is such a deeply ingrained belief that it feels like part of who they are. So when you expose them to love and caring, they flee. Why

shouldn't they? You are threatening to take away part of their identity, which would be threatening to anyone."

Lost identity? Borderline Personality? It all sounds so strange. I do have to admit that in all those years of treatment, you never lost your sense of humor, never ceased to worry about your father and me. On more than one occasion, you advised us, "Get counseling, Ma." But you know how it was in our family—we never talk about the important things.

When you returned to Arizona the next fall, you chose to ride your motorcycle, which you had purchased over the summer (with your own money). Was I happy about your decision? No. Should I have forbidden you?

"Are you crazy? I'd slash her tires! What are you thinking?" my friend Annie exclaimed.

What was I thinking? We were used to you making your own decisions. (Granny's words echo.) You were eighteen and capable. Is forbidding an adult offspring ever the right thing to do? There is a time to *let go and let live*. Scary! We knew our own fears for you, but did we ever know the fear within you? Your fa-çade fooled us all.

The rules were laid down: A call every night or I'd notify the police. With your camping map in hand, your gear piled high behind you, you set off under threatening black clouds piled high against the horizon. How far did you get before the deluge? You tell us of stopping beneath a bridge, a motorcycle that would not start until another cyclist stopped and lent a hand--a piece of foil in the fuse box—an ominous beginning!

(From LJ's journal)
It was my first motorcycle…a "chopper" Ma called it, with high reaching handle bars and a dual-level banana seat. Cute? Well it was what I wanted at the time. I made my plans and drew my maps carefully laying out my route to Arizona. Mother constantly said, "No." Dad was his quiet self and I kept on planning behind Mother's firm "No!"

I was going and so I did around the middle of August, a cold cloudy morning around 5:30 or 6:00 under the threat of rain. I took off, loaded to the hilt with tent, sleeping bag, tennis gear, and other miscellaneous crud. I got as far as Buffalo before I had total mechanical failure (a blown fuse compliments of my make-shift music system). In tears, I flagged down another motorcyclist (no car would stop) and shortly thereafter, with the help of some tin foil, I was on my way right into the rain which continued off and on for three days.

By New Mexico people quit gawking and exclaiming how terribly far I had to go. Camping out was an experience. The ground was hard but the tent went up quick and I was usually exhausted and slept well anyway. I made excellent mileage, 520 the first day, 730 the second, 500 the third and 620 the fourth. The trip totally added up to about 2500 to 2700 miles (the higher including a trip up to the Grand Canyon).

Rain? Of course, you did not turn back. I have often wondered what would have happened if I had gone with you on that trip to college riding on the back of your motorcycle, camping across country? It could have been the adventure of a lifetime for both of us, but there I go, *what-ifing* again.

When I arrived in Tucson, a girl I didn't know too well ran out with a big smile and a hug. Her name was Carrie Booth. She was a drama and dance major and was orga-nizing a skit for Rush. Rush went OK but I got bummed out one night…took the evening off…I started out as Carrie's secret admirer only to become best buddies…she kept me going and smiling. She brought me through some mighty rough times till finally I decided not even she was enough to make me stay. I bought some gear and at 4 AM one morning I took off on the bus for Colorado. From there I planned on walking, but after 10 miles was put between me and Cheyenne, well the thumb went out and I began my hitch hiking home.

Your college studies at the University of Arizona ended when you left suddenly during midterm, deciding to hitchhike home across country. It was a call from Sharon that alerted us that you were gone from school. Should we have called the police?

My first ride was a Catholic priest. A good sign? Yes, I guess so. He got on the phone. From then on it was truck-ers all the way. The first guy was an alcoholic chain smoker with an illegal overweight or length truck that wouldn't even pass inspection. We hauled grain. The next ride was a bit harder to get cuz a dog kept following me out of town, but I finally got it with a beanbag chair deliverer who was nice enough but eventually gave me a bit of a hassle, which, thank God, I got out of. Anyway I finally got home walking only the last three miles from the thruway exit.

Even though we had no idea where you were for several days, we waited. Worried? Of course, but you had always been very considerate, responsible. We waited through sleepless nights for your call—and then we saw you—huge back pack trudging down the road near home. Such relief! Could we just get out, grab you, and hug you? No! I was so angry and hurt, crazy from all the worry, so what did I say? "You want a ride or would you prefer to walk the rest of the way?"

Words, where were the words? Why couldn't we talk? You went to your room. We were expected for dinner at a friend's house. How could we? I know it sounds impossible, but I needed time to control the emotions that had been building for the past days of not knowing.

We thought we would give you time to unpack. We stayed only a short time then excused ourselves. You were gone when we returned. So where was the simple hug of relief that you were home safely, a quiet explanation of how worried we were about you, how frightened? It all seems so easy now, so wrong the way we handled it. You were almost twenty then.

This was before you lost your eye in the shooting, before your first suicide attempt, before you were declared *terminal* by the health gurus. *Terminal?* How insane was that? Did they know you, anything of what you had accomplished? I guess the real question was *did we know you*?

You returned to school and then left again. We received this rather frantic letter from Sharon, your close friend. What did she mean, *acting strangely*? We had yet to experience the full extent of your problems.

Dear Pat

You have no idea how hard it is for me to write you. I'm so sure I'll wake up tomorrow and it will be July again and none of this past semester would have occurred.

I'm really scared—I wonder if you understand why I love LauraJo so very much, at times I wonder if I haven't changed her and put the strain on her. So often I wonder where and why things went wrong and what (was it I) was causing this intense unhappiness.

You're right—it has been hard on me. But the pain becomes unbearable when I realize I'm not helping her or showing her how to work out these problems.

It also really tore me apart to realize after she came back that nothing had changed. She still had the same thoughts eating her apart. It's got to begin to change because we can only sweep over it so many times, until the moment it becomes too painfully real and it almost broke me apart the last few months. I was so afraid to tell you all so I told Jeff and let him make the decision to tell you all. You've got to talk it out…at least begin to conquer each small part of what's driving her to such extremes. I have almost realized these past few weeks that I cannot even be a friend if it all continues because it weakens me to the point of dropping out of everything.

...*I'd like to help....She worships you and that could be some of the problem....what type of relationship is workable for both of you...Where should I fit in...She's such a beautiful girl...don't mean to butt in...I'm so worried someday—be it tomorrow—she may not be around to help...*

Much, much love, Sharon

Chapter Eleven

Journal #1 The Khalil Gibran Diary for 1978

This diary was given to LJ from a friend she met at the University of Arizona 12/25/77 Inscribed as follows:

Dearest LauraJo:
This is a gift of sharing. Sharing a part of yourself with you. It means a great deal to me that you have this and treasure it throughout the new year. Write your beauties within its covers: your reflections on nature, God and the people you encounter each day. Use it as a friend, learn from it and you shall grow!

I can think of no other relationship that has withstood as much as ours, yet ours has blossomed with incredible beauty. Beauty like a red velvet rose or a purple shadowed cliff. Beauties so simple yet easily overlooked unless a passerby happens to pause and

> say, "Hey look! Aren't they beautiful?" Thank you, passerby, for becoming the friend that I have so often longed for. You are a part of me, as I am of you—this shall not ever be changed. May love & peace be yours forever. Carrie 'Boothy'

First Journal Entry

December 26, 1977 (LauraJo, age twenty)

January is coming. Today is the beginning of conviction, commitment and of sincere trying, for there is no tomorrow, only Now, so by each moment I will strive for improvement. Silently, for by experience I've felt the embarrassment of announced goals unfulfilled. It was enough to humble me for a while.

I feel a strong desire to communicate with Carrie, but it's unfair of me. She needs a more stable, happy person for a friend. I have too many ups and downs. It's a burden to a person…I think of her every day with gratitude and hope that we will someday get together again but the days are long and I have no future plans to pop in on her so this time it truly is up to God. I'm sure he'll do a better job of reuniting us than my hair brain schemes!

Thursday…2:00 AM.

As long as there is love there will be broken hearts and tears. Today Kurty (her younger brother) *is hurting with rejection for his love that has gone unreturned. I cryed for and with him today for I know the depth of sorrow. We went into the hills and climbed the giant oak. It was only 17 degrees, very cold, but nice to get outside.*

Mailed three letters, still no word from Carrie. Called her tonight after coming home from dancing around 1:00 AM. She was at a party. I'm glad to know she's having a good time. Hope she still thinks of me occasionally.

Sat morning…2:00 AM

…I just need someone to talk to. Called Carrie for the third time. She won't call back, really bugs me. Don't know what her problem is. Maybe she doesn't love me anymore or more so she's probably broke. I'd pay for the toll if only she'd call. Well, I won't call again, it's up to her now.

I try to play my guitar daily though sometimes like today when I worked 10 hrs, it's hard to work guitar in.

Tomorrow's the last day of Nov. Christmas will be here before I know it.

Sure hope Carrie answers my Thanksgiving letter. I must write Sharon too. All for now.

January 1, 1978

The moment has come and gone…it's just after twelve and I can hear people screaming. … called Carrie, though I shouldn't have, don't want to go crawling to anyone, not even my best friend. We talked for about 45 minutes. It was very good and happy. She's lost 6 lbs down to 131,

20 lbs less than me. I must catch up and reach her goal of 125 for that's a good goal for me too. I imagine me at 125, impossible? Never. Charge 250 calories per day, exercise, oh how glorious it would be. By my birthday, June 20, 125 lbs. I've been over weight for three years, time to Go for it! Yea!!! I love thin! Happy New Year. Oh, Carrie disapproves of Christian Science.

And what does a 151 lb girl eat to remain at this lovely weigh I shall tell you. This is for future reference, for unless it is sworn to in print I may never believe the hideous truth. Between the hours of 5:00 & 11:00 PM, in which I spent 4 hours teaching and traveling leaving 2 hours to eat, I put away:

½ bag potato chips (a big bag)
3 apples, 1 cup toffee covered peanuts, 15 chocolate chip cookies
1 inch slice beef stick, 1 cup peanut M&Ms
2 pieces of bread
½ cucumber
Slice cheese
1 cracker
a pickle
a cup of broth
2 melba thins
4 oranges

And that's all I can recall. Seems impossible doesn't it? Oh how I wish it were. I'm definitely a food alcoholic. It is terrible. I find myself sneaking food and feeling terribly guilty yet doing it all the same. I make promises to myself I know I can't keep and it seems to get worse every day. I'm getting desperate. It's humiliating to be seen in public. Oh, woe is me. I'm miserable…& it's my own damn fault!

May 13, 1978, PM

Observation LJE: The painful and difficult times of our lives are merely the adventurous tales when the misery and hurt are forgotten.

I often wonder if life merits a question with all of its incon-sistencies. Could there be an answer or must we merely accept it like a tree accepts the wind, bending and moan-ing, singing a song of loneliness to the night? And yet the questions are as a spring from the hillside ever bubbling forth pushed outward from within by some unseen force. There must be a reason; a purpose yet if satisfaction lies in finding it, then there shall be none. And so for peace of mind we must be as the tree in the night, bending and ac-cepting and being in this manner strong.

You ask the question that hovers in all of our minds: "What's the point--life?" From the Khalil Gibran Diary

Desire for Life

And when you were a silent word upon life's quivering
Lips, I too was there, another silent word.
Then Life uttered us and we came down the years
Throbbing with memories of yesterday and with
Longing for tomorrow, for yesterday was death
Death conquered and tomorrow was birth pursued.

Chapter Twelve

June 1, 1978

*Well now its June 1st, PM and I have just picked out my car, a Fiat **X** 1/9. Now, "Will I get it?" that's the question. Dad and I are going to look at it again tomorrow afternoon. See what he thinks. I also saw an ad for a $75 Junker. It runs, supposedly.*

DRIVERS

You blow your horn and cut me off
I want to swear and kick,
But being mad feels awfully bad
So I think on God a bit.
(First) I ask him for a thunderbolt
To blow your car apart,
Then thinking twice I ask Him nice
For understanding in my heart.
So maybe if I knew just why
You act like such a jerk,
I'd trade the thunderbolt
For simply ice cubes down your shirt.

But I am only human
Far from perfect and trying hard
To love you despite your actions
And keep from ramming your blankity blank car!

June 4, 1978, 11:00 PM

Life is good. I'm grabbing it by the tail and taking a ride. Weeeeeeeee Haaaaaaaaa. I'm really having a ball with Sue and Peg. They're great. It's nice to have friends again, and try new things (bong.) Mostly I like laughing w/them. They are pretty and thin and great to be with me. I'm just "sturdy" and have fun.

REFLECTIONS

You sit before me
My friend of new.
I look into your eyes.
Beyond that smile
To see a part of me,
An image, a reflection
Traits I long to acquire.
Respect and love
Make me smile.

How many times does a young bird fall from the nest be fore succeeding in a few brief seconds of flight? Yet he keeps trying until he is there, airborne, suspended. Free from all which held him.

I want to fly but I keep falling, each time from a greater height. I long to try everything, to enjoy everything, to live and love so very freely that there is no room for hurt. It seems I often wait so long for love yet when it comes, it is boundless and strong. Deep in all manner of devotion and I dare not keep it inside lest I burst. Like a steam welling within the earth, it builds, wanting to rush forth and swallow that which calls it from without. Yet without caution or in haste the scalding vapor could kill when it only searches to woo and comfort. Holding back love in frustration and worry is vexatious to the soul, a burden that weighs day by day heavier.

How many loves have I killed with this very rush? This overpowering strength, meaning no harm, only going by my feelings. I often wonder if I am doomed to this perpetual heartache for I cannot go slow. I am driven by a deep seeded need for companionship and love, and like a miser and his money, I never have enough.

LJ, following are the thoughts about love from your favorite philosopher:

At the Door of the Temple
Khalil Gibran

I purified my lips with the sacred fire to speak of love
But when I opened my lips I found myself speechless,
Before I knew love, I was won't to chant the songs of love,
But when I learned to know, the words in my mouth
Became naught save breath,
And the tunes within my breast fell into deep silence.

June 20, 1978 (*My 21st birthday*)

Observations LJE: Forever is the eternity it takes to utter the word...never is as long as it is convenient.

I must say that this has been one of the greatest days in my life. Suzanne has been my salvation, my joy, my entire life and there are not enough good words in this world for her. She is kind, loving, beautiful and best of all my best friend. She has given me more than she'll ever know. If only I was capable of telling her how very much she fills my every need. Joy is being with her in silence and conversation, in laughter and in tears. She believes in me, she loves me and makes me believe in myself. We will be friends forever. Near or far here and after. Lord look after her. She doesn't believe she is a gem, a jewel rare and perfect. May love and kindness follow her all the days of her life and may we share many, many years together as the close friends (more really) that we are!

For "Farrah" (Suzanne though I'll never
have the nerve to give it to her)

You're the silent laughter of sunshine
The joy of a newborn life.
You're flowers dancing all in a line
You're notes from a minstrel's fife.
You're the beautiful blush
Of a budding rose
A cooling breeze where
The evergreen grows.
The moon through the trees
On a cloudless night,
The sun on the wings
Of a bird in flight
Yet more than these
You're a special friend
One to whom
My love I send. (LauraJo)

June, 1978,10:00 PM

Observation LJE: If it came down to trying harder there might be a chance, yet it seems to be something far beyond mere trying.

Sue puts it very well, "What right have you to be unhappy? You're talented, loved, & well off, so cut it out or I'll give you a karate chop."

Maybe that's what I need. A good kick in the pants but I do try. I try to convince myself everything couldn't be better but at night, alone in my room that old ache returns, that hateful hollow feeling that leaves a knot in my stomach and a thorn in my heart. What is it I want damn it. Any person would give their eyeteeth to have what I have. I hate myself even more for not being as happy as a lark. I must be ready for the nut house not to be walking around with a smile 24 hrs a day. "What's wrong LJ? Where are you these days? What are you thinking?"…quit quoting movies….

June, 1978

Dear Diary:

*How's that for a start? Today I'm going to be straight with you. **I don't care if someone reads it someday** because when I look back on this I want to see the truth, all of it not half. I was out till 2:00 AM this morning talking with "Farrah." It was so hard at first. I felt uncomfortable trying to explain how very lonely I felt at the thought of not seeing her anymore.*

She's my only friend presently and like the friends in my past, I care very much for her. I'd like to forget about the past and all its disappointments but those from within are hard to forget. Sue is so giving. She's like no one I've ever met. I don't know why I told her so much of my past and my strong death wish but she kept asking and maybe I felt if I told her the gorey details she'd say, "Hey, no way, this kid's too much for me to handle." And then it would be over and I could cry a bit, add another hurt to the list and go on living…alone.

I'm so terrible sometimes in what I say. It's like a test—see how much you can lay on before you lose a friend. It's hardly their fault. I mean they're human and vulnerable too. But Sue didn't quit on me. She hung on and was strong and filled me with hope where I thought there couldn't be any more. She told me how much we were alike and how she wouldn't let me down and though I've believed that line from everyone in the past, thinking how different it was going to be this time, I dare to say maybe it's true. Maybe it's my 21st B day present from the Lord. A real friend, a lasting friend, one the months or even years won't take away. Sue is as beautiful on the inside as she is on the outside and I am blessed to call myself her friend. I don't ever want to do anything that would hurt her and I will not be the destructive force anymore. I will give through it all and take only as much as I can put out. I will love until it ceases to hurt anymore and when the end comes, for this thing I won't be sorry.

If I had a prayer to give now it would be to ask God for the strength of heart that a lasting friendship requires, the patience, love and generosity necessary for two halves to become a whole or even greater for two individuals to share and at times be one. The task is unending but the reward is a bit of heaven on earth. It is joy, peace. It is grace.

Chapter Thirteen

June,1978

What is wrong? How many times have they asked me? How many times have I asked me? Damn, I'm losing. This thing is weighing on me like a morning fog in the valley. If only some wind would stir the murk. Give me some small sign of life. I don't want to lose. Too many people I love will be hurt. Mom, who through all her tough exterior is one of the most tender, sincere, giving people I know. She loved me like the mother of her dreams, the mother *she never had, the friend she always wanted and I loved her back just as strongly, and though now through many painful but maturing years I can see her as the woman she really is. A woman with faults like any human being but also a lonely woman, frustrated that she can't seem to help her only daughter whom she loves dearly. Oh Mom, if only for you and Dad I would try to stop hurting, stop doing things you don't understand nor do I.*

God, why? Why do I have so much if my near future will only take it away? Why can't I live for today, happy or at least at peace?

LJ, so much of your time was spent imagining your death...why not life?

The Art of Happiness. Throughout your journals, LJ, you seek happiness, an elusive dream to us all. The following article is from a magazine called *ODE* interviewing The *Professor of Happiness,* Christopher Andre. When asked: "Do you think people are naturally happy?" His reply:

"We tend to be naturally gloomy. Melancholy is LA CONDITION HUMAINE. Biologically oriented psychologists agree there's a good evolutionary reason for this. When we were all still hunters and gathers, a certain degree of concern was useful. It was prudent to remain alert to dangers and problems, which is why we're geared to focus on the negative. It appears that the Christian church understood this early on: *There's no point looking for happiness on earth; heaven is where you'll find it.* It is the reason why Sigmund Freud wrote: *Happy is not included in the plan of creation. It is proven that happiness and unhappiness are registered in different parts of the brain.*

"And parents don't often teach their children about happiness. Have you ever been on vacation and seen them stop the car, point, and say: *Look what a beautiful mountain valley. See that old tree and how beautifully it's catching the light?* They're more focused on how well their children are doing in school."

The following list is his advice about how to attain happiness. I read them and try to remember.

SIX LESSONS FOR A HAPPIER LIFE

1. Accept that there will be unpleasant things in life. All the time, every day. You'll face hindrances: You'll be too late or make a mistake or say something stupid, it's the rent you pay to live in the house of life, it's part of life. There's no point in being disappointed when things don't go your way.

2. Open your eyes and look around. There are more opportunities for happiness than you think, certainly for a Westerner in 2008. Embrace the moments. Try to remember them. Enjoy them.

3. Take time out. The ability to pause, mentally as well as in your actions, is important. Taking breaks is a prerequisite for experiencing happiness.

4. Pay attention to your family and friends. Social ties are important to happiness. Don't let a day go by without thinking of, or seeing, someone you love.

5. Try to get in touch with nature every day. Take a walk in the park and spend a few minutes looking at nature.

6. Express your gratitude and respect for the good things you experience. Being thankful makes you happy and increases the chance of social connection.

The irony of it all is that you practiced many of the above suggestions. I think back. It seems that you were always striving to prove something. You excelled in so many areas, athletics, music, art, scholastics, but it never seemed enough; you were always seeking. If your father and I had praised you more, would it have made a difference? Were we that hard to please? I realize that children are always seeking their parents' approval. It never occurred to us that you didn't know how proud we were of you and your brothers, but then I remember Spike, our family friend and tennis pro, saying, "Do you realize how talented your children are?" If our lack of praise was evident to an outsider, the three of you surely must have missed it.

I watch your brothers. Kurt's family celebrates every stepping stone in their children's lives. Could more applause have truly been the answer?

June, 1978

Everyone is trying to help. Dad, such a quiet man, yet for the first time in my life I see the love in his eyes, I hear the concern in his voice. So generous, thoughtful, and in his own way, affectionate...

An early spring raft trip

Still another adventure shared with your father and older brother, Jeff. An early spring raft trip down the Hudson River... you all about died of frostbite!

"Whose bright idea was this?" rang your father's voice, echoing his discomfort. Life seemed so normal. The following is an unsung song you wrote to your Dad...your voice echoes.

I wish I could have held you
When you were just a boy
And said the words, "I love you, Son,
You are my pride and joy."
But I cannot be your father lost
Who died when you were young
And left you with a broken heart
Alone with songs unsung.
Who am I but your only daughter
Wanting earnestly to say
I've so much love to give you
For now and yesterday.
A gentle man of so few words
I wish you'd talk to me.
I want desperately to know you
Father, you are a part of me.
Oh, Father, please forgive me
If I've ever been cruel.
It's time to open up our hearts
It's time for love's renewal.

June, 1978 (cont.)

I don't want to hurt them. Not Mom, Dad, or Kurt with his deep insight and gentle way. His imagination was always the wild and free. We were everything from soldiers in the jungle to stranded seafarers surrounded by peronakeets. And Jeff who, with his easy going manner and constant stream of interesting conversation, seems to make every-one feel at ease. Of all the family, he seems to know exactly where he's going and what he wants. What he starts gets finished on time and with a quality he can be proud of. And though his handwriting is a bit scribbely, when love fills his heart, he's another Walt Whitman. Some woman should consider herself very lucky to snag such a prize!

I look at the picture from babies to adults. I remember the years. Life was good. We laughed, we loved—one for all and all for one!

June, 4:00 PM

Getting back to right now. I am in Granny's condo at Georgetown Commons. I now have my own car after a generous $1600 loan from Granny and a summer of clean- ing a store (AM) and teaching tennis late ($3100 in only the car. It only took Travers 3 months to fulfill their part of the bargain and threats of court proceedings from me. What a pleasant time that all was. Shit! And that's putting my frustrations lightly since it is presently inoperable now with a disconnected throttle cable...again!

Enough about that silly car. It frustrates me just thinking about it. I'd like to expound on Granny for a moment: One of the most daring, changing, brave women I ever met or been privileged to be related to. So level headed and busi- ness like. I don't ever know how she loaned me $1600 but she showed me some trust and I proved myself by paying it back in less than 3 months. I think the most surprised person around was me. I never thought I'd live through it and I mean that literally. Oh well, I made it and I'm still here, though I don't know for how long.

And so the battle within you raged. Should I have known with all those motorcycles, the parachuting, repelling, scuba diving? Self destructive? I thought, *adrenalin junkie.* Were you running away from life or running toward death? But these were all subtle signs. And then began the real thing: the carbon monoxide, poison, pills, knives for cutting flesh and ropes for hanging, and the trip to Niagara Falls. Remember? Your frantic and tearful telephone call, "Ma, the wheel fell off my car!" you sobbed. Sorry about the laughter, LJ, but by this time I knew why you had gone—the falls, so inviting, so dramatic!

"Don't you understand, Ma? I could have been killed! The irony of your words echoed.

But perhaps I get ahead of myself. The memories tumble about in my head with no time line, no order. Was Granny right? Was I that careless of a mother? Cause, what was the cause? Could it have been the stories I shared with you of my growing up? The dark moments remain buried, but maybe the trivial, funny/scary adventures? The break in the canal washing away our house--could that have been the cause? I search for clues.

Chapter Fourteen

September 22, 1978, Friday, 8:00 PM

Three whole months have passed since I last recorded my thoughts. So very much has changed. So many new experiences have filled my days and nights. Good and bad or perhaps better labeled as—the wrinkles of life.

Sue and I have been together almost constantly since we met. She is very special, very strong and faithful. Our sharing has brought us extremely close, almost as though we were part of one another. I love her and she me. Her fortitude has brought me thru many a hardship...tranquilizers, cooking spray, and countless very low moments.

It is hard to fathom our relationship, especially for Mom and Dad who, like most people, have a set idea of how married people should act and what routes a marriage should follow. There's nothing wrong with their ideas, I only wish they could realize that theirs is not the only way, though I must admit they have been very successful.

I love them dearly, even through all our disagreements and lack of communication. They are my parents and no matter what they say or do, I'll always know in my heart that it is because they love me. I honestly believe that there could not possibly be a more loved person in this world than myself. My gifts are many and varied. My opportunities at times seem limitless.

Why then is there this ache, this dull/sharp yet ever constant pain in my heart. Often it's almost as though I'm fighting within myself: Someone or something is trying to steal me away from the happiness I once knew. It is something evil and powerful and there are times when I simply cannot win over it. It turns all hope into a dismal future. It drains the joy from a sunny spring morning and fills my every waking hour with the longing for death. I have so so much and this thing within is trying to throw it all away like I never mattered and never will.

September 28, 1978

I want it to look like an accident but in thinking about it, how could anyone with an I.Q. over 60 die of carbon monoxide poisoning accidently? I just think it would hurt them less if they thought it was an accident. For like everyone else, all they see is how very much I have going for me. A good job, a nice house, loving friends and family. Besides what else could anyone want or need? Nothing, absolutely nothing. I've got everything. More than one person deserves, more talent than one person needs, more love than one person could ask for, so what's wrong? **What's wrong!** *Damn it! All I know is that I'd give up half my talents, all my possessions and some of my love just to have some peace of mind, some goal and purpose to my life, some answers to all my unanswered questions.*

Mom is trying to help the best she knows how; by trying to find me 10 hrs. of work a day. Maybe she's right, maybe "idleness is the devil's playground," but from my experience in the past it just doesn't work. Take for instance school at U of A. My last semester I sure was busy with 25 units and I did alright, averaging along at about a 3.0, but all that busyness just made it worse, and so I ran. It didn't matter where to, but I ended up at home where nothing seemed to improve. I ache for my family and friends. They don't know what to do. Mom tries to keep me busy. Dad tries to be understanding and patient.

Kurt and Jeff encourage me and Granny tries to tell me to hang in there and reminds me of how much I have going for me. They are all so precious to me.

I don't want to leave them. I don't want to die. I'm so afraid. I love life so much. The seasons, the storms, the ever-beautiful, ever-changing land. I don't want to go away. It's so lonely and dark out there. It's so unknown, but what can I do? I can't just stop working and be a sluff. I can't run away again. I know in my present state I can't go to school in the winter. I've tried shrinks. We either don't get along or they dump me because they are too busy.

I can't teach tennis when my insides are eating themselves out. I can't seem to do anything. It's hard enough to get out the front door in the morning and yet no one can ever know the torment I feel the constant battle I fight just to stay alive. Something in me, something evil wants me to die, but there is me in there too and I want to live, and no matter how close the evil gets I always seem to stagger through, at least so far. So far I have been victorious, sick a lot but not dead. No one but Sue knows that I have been in the hospital twice this summer and out of work 4 times now due to "battle wounds" if I may call them that.

I am so afraid that the enemy is winning. My alternatives are few if any. I can't troop home and say I don't want to work, I don't want to play, just let me sit in the corner. Mom would try to understand but would continue with her busy-bee remedy, only because she loves me, and we all resort to what we believe will work. Dad would ship me off to the R-wing and who knows, maybe that would help? Jeff and Kurt would say, "Shape up, count your blessings and be happy. After that, get to work." I'll tell you honestly if I could do the first part the second would be only natural.

I've won a lot in my life but I've also lost a few. This is one I can't afford to lose. It's a deadly game, this life and death struggle. I have so very much to lose but unfortunately, that fact doesn't always assure victory. If I should lose I have but one wish, that you will not think less of me as a human being for you, my family, know more than anyone else what a fighter I am and if by chance victory alludes my grasp you must believe I tried; I really tried. I gave it my all and I love you for sticking by me. You're more than I ever deserved. And if life's road is vacant one spot once filled by me, please just close your ranks and be strong in the face of hardship. After all, you're still a family, we're still a family. Be strong, be brave, and stay with me. Always.

September 28, 1978
Friends

My friend, Suzanne, more than I could pray for, how can I save you from the hurt I cause you. You go through it all while everyone else carries on in blissful ignorance. You cry, hurt and grieve as I do. It is so unfair to you, so cruel am I, to continue to do this. If I loved you enough I would throw you out, breaking your heart but saving your soul, but I am selfish. I love your companionship. I thrive on your love for me.

I'm too selfish to turn that away, but when I see your vacant, sad helpless eyes I know what I must do. I know I must send you away. I must hurt you now to save you later. I can't bear the thought of you being in pain. I'm sorry. I'm sorry. And though that does no good, there is little else for me to say except I love you. I really do. And I said once before, if you must hate me to survive then do it. For God's sake do it, but most importantly do what I am failing. Survive!

Health

There is another thing I don't understand: Disease. It seems in this day and age to be classified an illness or disease to the general public one must have visible, physical symptoms, such as cancer. Here we have an oftentimes fatal disease where the symptoms are quite visible both by x-ray and in later stages, the human eye. When death occurs, everyone is very sorry for the poor person who could, of course, do nothing about their disease.

Now, hypothetically, we have a person being consumed by an invisible disease. One which works away at its host not unlike a parasite. It causes strange reactions to what may seem normal situations. It causes distress, sadness, discontent, confusion, indecision, and in severe cases— death. Now do people look on and say…"Oh poor fellow. Not a thing he could do." No. They don't. No they look on, and seeing no physical symptoms, they say, "Look what that stupid fool did to himself. I mean look at all the things that guy had going for him. A gorgeous wife, nice kids, good home, great job. Why in the hell did he go and do a dumb thing like that for?"

Of course, the person with cancer had a nice wife, great kids, beautiful home so why did he up and die? Tell me that. Why did that stupid fool let the disease win?

Now they'll say: That second guy didn't have a disease. Hell, he was just sitting around feeling sorry for himself. And for what reason? He had a great... and so on and so on. I don't want sympathy. Maybe only for my family and those I love, but not for me, though I honestly believe now that I do have a disease and it is killing me. I don't want any body's "Oh poor girl." Save it for a more deserving soul. Try to understand. Not for me but for yourselves, for your peace of mind, for I may never have any. I may be forced to search for eternity for something I was never meant to find.

I only pray that the peace I lack you may all know either now or very soon. And may it stay with you for eternity. My weight is still unforgivably atrocious, 152 lbs before tonight's pork out. I am ashamed, and let down. It's so very hard. That's all for tonight.

Weight

This country is now in a widespread battle with obesity. Billions of dollars every year are spent on the newest book or the latest fad diet. Almost every magazine has the latest scoop on how to lose ten pounds in ten minutes! One of the most well-known celebrities, Oprah Winfrey, yoyos up and down in spite of all the money in the world and her own personal athletic trainer. You had your charts.

The many months you spent incarcerated in one hospital after another changed your lifestyle from a true athlete, to one of inactivity. We became aware of a pattern—your binging appeared to be symptomatic of an imbalance within your body, an effort to ward off some hidden foe. We watched and knew when the blackness was overcoming you—a dozen donuts at a sitting... sugar. In your growing years fruit had always been your preference. This dietary change was evident.

Twenty years ago, weight was a cosmetic goal to mimic models and actresses. Today, we have become aware of the health risks. The government is stepping up its crusade on obesity. At their insistence, schools are changing menus. Awareness of the health costs and diminished life style has moved to the forefront.

Obese? In your mind. Throughout your ordeal, your clothes were never larger than a size 14. Was it too simple to think the added weight was from a changed life style? The physical exercise of an athlete changed to the inactivity of one living in institution after institution, and who knows how the emotional distress and medication wrought its changes in your physical being.

Always dieting, binging, fasting. I remember the time when you were living at home. You never seemed to join us for dinner, always *busy*. We tried to honor your independence and didn't insist. How little we look at each other—blind to the day-to-day differences.

How long did it take me to see what was happening? Two weeks? How many pounds had you shed? Your naturally round face was actually becoming gaunt. One of many *fasting* episodes. Not exactly anorexia, but an obsession stimulated by your and society's love affair with *thin*.

Chapter Fifteen

First recorded suicide attempt

October 2, 1978

I don't remember why I went over to Granny's that day, LJ. I tried to call. We wanted to take you out for dinner. I didn't feel any apprehension, just thought I might catch you between jobs and errands. The garage door was our entry into Granny's back court-yard. Did I smell the fumes?

It was evident that you had tried to abort your effort, for you hung half in half out of the car. Your note, which was more to Suzanne than to us, was on the mantle. It became part of the police report.

Those first days are folded back deep into my memory closet. I haven't taken them out for years. I remember the seizures and the doctor's prognosis...we didn't need words to see in his face that your chances were slim, that the damage would be great, that your mental capacity would be impaired. For two days you shuddered between life and death. On that third day, after only a few hours of being conscious—what relief to see your hazel-green eyes open to the world—I hugged you, then held you away from me, and I can't believe *almost* the first words out of my mouth: "What's your social security number, LJ?" Out tumbled the numbers without a moment's hesitation. You were fully back!

October 22, 1978

This is the first chance I've had to write since Oct. 2nd when I shut myself into the garage for 6 hrs. with the car running. They (the doctors) classified it as a miraculous recovery after only four days in the intensive care I was ready to check out! I guess they thought I'd probably be a vegetable, that is if I lived, and they had their doubts about that.

October 23, 1978

The last thing I remember it was the 2nd of Oct. around noon. I suppose and I had decided against doing it since I tried to get out but didn't make it. The next thing I knew I was waking up Wed. afternoon in intensive care. I didn't even know what had happened, but it all started to come back later. I guess I was in a coma for a while and the only way they could get a reaction from me was by jabbing needles into me. Susie said I'd have seizures where I'd stiffen up and shake all over and it looked like I'd die right there and then. I was on the critical list for two days but as of Wednesday Oct. 4th, it was uphill all the way. All the tubes and needles came out by Wednesday evening and I was ready to leave by Friday, but due to lack of beds in R Wing (psychiatric wing), I didn't leave till Saturday. They were real nice to me there but I was glad to leave. Not so glad to go to R-Wing though. That was the pits. There I met Char and Pat, my nurses. We had a lot of long talks, and two terribly boring weeks later I got to leave. It wasn't quite so bad when Dr. Sobel let me on B limits. Then at least I could go outside by myself. I even snuck off limits into Mt. Hope Cemetery where I spent many hours looking at grave stones wondering how it would have been if one had been mine.

November 5, 1978, 11:00 PM

Observation LJE: I pray the lord will help me to understand that frustrating, out-of-character version of himself in the Old Testament.

I came back today, as Susie said. Meaning I was once again the girl she first loved and met. There was enthusiasm in my voice, a zest for life, a twinkle in my eye. And of what am I speaking? Why of course, my relationship with God.

I've at last begun to realize the strength of His love for me. The power of His guiding light and once again I asked Him to take control of my life to make me what He wants me to be, but I must say that God alone is worth living for and the precious life He's given me. Praise His holy name. Amen.

Concern for Granny

LJ, your concern for the family remained strong throughout your journey. You had negotiated with Granny on several occasions in buying your car and renting her apartment. The guilt you felt for breaking her trust by attempting suicide in her home is evident in the letter you wrote trying to explain.

November 16, 1978

Dear Granny,

Thank you for writing back so promptly. I was worried you wouldn't write at all, but that's what's so special about you. You can forgive. I guess my greatest problem has been in not being able to forgive myself. Sometimes it just seems too hard, and now, when I think about my reasons for what I did they don't seem so very horrible, though it is a fear which shall be with me for a long time. More now a question than a fear.

It is hard when I have to ask myself what I am sexually; when I have to ask myself why I've always felt closer to women than men? I've had to fight the ridicule my whole life. Ridicule for being a Tom Boy, for not going along with peer pressure in some areas. Yet more than the comments such as "thing" was the exclusion I felt. I'm not sorry I never dated because I really wasn't that interested and I guess that's what increased my doubts about myself. Yet my love for my female friends was always so innocent, that was until the first day of October '78.

I am 21! There must be something there, mustn't there? Those feelings everyone had always said were the most exciting, thrilling feelings one could ever have come to me in the company of another woman. It wasn't so much what we did, for we had always given each other back rubs and foot rubs, but it was the way I felt at this particular time. It was nice and I felt so ashamed and guilty. I felt I had committed a sin against myself and God.

I don't think I'm a lesbian anymore but being one of my first experiences with those kinds of feelings, I thought I might be and what a wretched thought that was. An unacceptable thought. To be dead would be better...then it seemed so.

Now I'm hoping that is not true. I'm praying that even if this is the case with me, I will be able to accept myself and continue to experience the many joys life has to offer. After all...I did make an effort to get out of the car and *that internal desire for life is what I believe pulled me thru it all so quickly and so well.*

My soul would have been just as troubled after death as before, for killing the body can't kill the soul. God saved me from an eternity of misery and searching. He's given me a second chance and I must work to deserve it, to thank him for it.

I go to Sobel about once every ten days. She is expensive: $60 for 45 minutes and my insurance won't cover it. There are other bills coming in to which Blue Cross finds outs on. I'm only earning about $120 a week at my two jobs and if I'm going to swing school in January I may have to quit seeing Sobel.

Believing in God's plan for my life seems to help the most anyway. Also a big part is a family that cares so much. I love you and hope you can understand what I've tried to say.

Love LJ

Chapter Sixteen

Granny born August 2, 1909

About Granny: Granny was a flapper! The youngest and only one of nine children to graduate from high school. Married three times: buried two, divorced one.

"I gave him eight years…he never bought a loaf of bread! I'll not marry again, I'm not about to take care of an old man, but a 'Sugar Daddy' would be nice!" Her words echo.

One might think she was a real swinger, but actually she was a quiet, soft-spoken woman, a non-interfering mother-in-law, independent and adventurous in her own way—riding on the back of your motorcycle, going down the rapids on our camping trips, even though she couldn't swim. She was conservative and thrifty with her money, a diehard Republican, and a stickler for punctuality. I used to have ulcers, trying to get you kids in the car and get to her house *on time.*

Your letter speaks so respectfully of her as you would, but are we able to touch our true feelings with pen in hand, or is it in the spoken words when they tumble forth wrapped in the emotions uncontrolled by social rules of *nice?* You and Granny had less than a wonderful relationship. You baited each other—the sarcasm dripping—about her organ playing from you, about your selfishness from her.

After you were grown, I spoke to her of your and Jeff's contentious relationship. She expressed her opinion, "You were so partial to her, spoiling her, always taking her side over Jeff's" (her favorite).

Granny took her disapproval of me and my actions out on you, as we adults are prone to do. How easy to make these judgments when we are not privy to a family's dynamics, when we haven't seen the interaction between family members. How could she know how annoyed I got with you when you played the *not-fair* card, or how I had to step in when Jeff hit you to protect you from physical harm, even though you may have instigated his response? Was it that trip to her home in Michigan when you were ten—your teary voice begging, "Can I come home, Mom? I love Granny, but I'm used to you."

Was that when your relationship grew prickly? Or were your relationship problems so simply explained? Granny always treated you equally with gifts, but I could never forget her words, "I just don't like her!" What brought out those words from a soft-spoken woman who rarely voiced her opinion and never criticized my *parenting* skills?

Her comment after that first suicide attempt: "She's just spoiled!" Have I ever been able to forgive her in my heart for that, or not coming to your funeral, her only granddaughter? But I get ahead of myself.

Religion

> **Prayer: LJE That I follow faithfully God's guidance in my life, wherever He leads, to follow; and whatever He instructs, to do. I pray for the assurance that where I go is where the Lord wants me to go; for no confusion or doubt regarding His wishes.**

God gave me another chance. He could have taken me or even worse, left me a vegetable mentally and with physical damage to my nerves, but He didn't. It seems I'm nearly as good as new except for poor endurance and stamina, but that will come if I keep up my jogging.

I've asked myself so many times, "Am I glad to be alive?" And though still at times I'm lonely and depressed, I have to say yes and thank you for another chance. There must be a reason, for all probability was against me. They gave little hope of my ever functioning again. Was it some miraculous intervention that returned me to my life? Whatever, here I am. Someone up there must want me around and I had better quit tempting Him, quit playing the odds. I don't think He'll put up with all my games for long.

I must believe. I must have faith, for there have been the times when I have held fast to my belief and He's always come thru. Though in truth I deserve no favor. no miracles. I can't help but say why me? Why am I so fortunate? Maybe I'm never to know and besides why should I need to? Isn't it enough to know He loves me and is willing to give me another chance? 2nd chances are rare.

My gratitude knows no bounds. I humble myself before you, Lord, forgive my actions, help to make me more worthy of your love.

Oh Ye of Little Faith

"See, Mom, I told you!" There was a triumphant look on your face as you shook the check under my nose. It all started when you came home from Arizona, finals hanging in the wind, without your motorcycle. You had sold it to a young man, but he couldn't pay for it right away, he promised a check later.

"You didn't give him the title did you?"

"Well, sure, how could he license it without the title?"

"Don't hold your breath until you see that money!" I shook my head at your blind trust.

"You're such a cynic, Mom. Of course he's going to pay me."

The check was supposed to arrive in June. I'd forgotten all about it until I noticed you picking up the mail every day. I didn't say anything. What was there to say? The days passed on into July. One day you came in, flushed with triumph. As you shook his check in my face, you explained, "He's sorry he's late, but a friend needed the money for a couple of weeks." Your belief has never ceased to amaze me. Throughout your life you gave—tithed—no matter how little you had. And money would always appear: $25 from Granny who rarely sent you money except on holidays, or your birthday, a request for a private tennis lesson, a racquet stringing job, or lawn mowing opportunity. The good Lord provided.

Your belief remained strong throughout your life experiences. I remember your comment during one of your stays at home when you went door-to-door with your religious *message.* "Is my nose shorter, Ma?" Even the door slamming didn't discourage you. Could prayer make a difference? Unlike me, you never asked. Does religion make you a better person?

Your faith made me wonder, thus the letter from Norman Vincent Peale's office responding to a letter I had written.

FOUNDED 1628

MARBLE COLLEGIATE CHURCH
FIFTH AVENUE AT 29TH STREET, WEST
NEW YORK, N. Y. 10001
212.686.2770

NORMAN VINCENT PEALE
ARTHUR CALIANDRO
Ministers

STANERT L. DRANSFIELD, D. D.
Associate Minister

June 7, 1983

Mrs. Pat Engebrecht
20 Lodge Pole Road
Pittsford, New York 14534

Dear Mrs. Engebrecht:

Our hearts go out in love to Laura Jo and to all of you
in her family as you say your prayers and stand beside her
in her life/death struggle. When reason fails and medical
and psychological tests seem inconclusive, we return to
the place we began - "Dear God, help!"

How I wish that I had some wise words with which to comfort
and reassure you. Or some miraculous power that I could
use to ease Laura Jo's pain and lift your burden. What I do
have is a firm conviction that God loves your daughter, and
that "underneath are the everlasting arms" of His mercy.

I recently wrote out my thoughts on prayer to use in a sermon
here this summer. I wonder if it would help you as you reaffirm your faith in the Infinite Power and love of God.

Sincerely,

Stanert L. Dransfield
Stanert L. Dransfield

SLD:cw

The response? Seven pages of examples of his personal experience with prayer. He notes that some requests were granted, although not as he expected, and those that never happened: recovery from illness of a dear friend, a job opportunity that never materialized, for happiness and peace of mind, for love he accepted *His* will. *Have faith* was his advice, plus many quotations from the good book admonishing the same thing.

Observation LJE: I still think the most glorious church God has ever created is the still hush of a dew-laden morning. The spider webs sparkle like decorative ornaments on a lighted Christmas tree and the sunbeams make me catch my breath and silently praise the Creator. The morning is crisp and the effort feels good as I peddle my bicycle up and down the rolling hills, making a circle toward home.

Throughout your ordeal you never ceased believing in God's goodness, in his love, but your reaction to Dr. Peal's ending his advice with a story about a young woman who became paralyzed but went on to overcame her injuries by painting beautiful pictures with her teeth left you with anger. You hated stories like that—the super human person who rose above the greatest of odds to triumph over life's challenges. What was meant to inspire, discouraged: "It makes me feel that it is my fault, that my faith is lacking, that if my belief was strong enough, I could get past this." I continue to search for the point, the point in all your suffering. Within Peale's essay on prayer I read the following: *In Christ's prayer of desperation, "Save me!" But He added what must be added spoken or unspoken, to every prayer: "Nevertheless,* not my will but Thine be done"…when His mission required the *ultimate sacrifice, He said to his disciples, "The cup that my father has given me, shall I not drink of it?"*

And drink you did, LJ. Who's to say that the answer wasn't the added years of sharing your talents, writings, songs, compassion with fellow travelers? You touched so many lives along your way. You believed! Never doubting throughout all your suffering! Through it all, your love for the Lord's creation was ever in your heart...

Chapter Seventeen

November 29, 1978

Well I suppose it's time for another entry in the ol diary. So very much has happened since my last entry over three weeks ago.

The bad new first…It happened again. Don't ask what. You should know. Only this time it went further. Much further and it mustn't happen again. At least until I know what I am or want to be. I have to get away from Sue for there is no half way with her, either because of her or me or more than likely both of us.

It's going to hurt so much. Argggghhhh! She'll say she understands but she won't. It's just too much right now. Too much.

Observation LJE: Bear the pain, it will not last for joy is sorrow's child.

Tonight was really a milestone. I was frustrated, confused, Ma tells me this, Sue tells me the opposite. They're both at their own extreme. I'm sick of all the pressure though they'll both surely deny any intent at pressuring me. I love them both. Anyway, back to the point. Instead of hurting myself and clamming up tonight, I called Pat and we talked. Then I went out and ran. Into the hills I went and there, where only the grass could hear me, I screamed at the top of my lungs. It felt a little embarrassing but good too. I asked God what to do. Only the wind answered. Cold and alone, I wondered where that promised peace was. That peace that passeth all understanding.

Tomorrow I talk to Sobel. No matter what she says, I've decided there will be no trip to Toronto. Susie knows, but I must tell her.

So much for all the heavy stuff. Now for a look on the lighter side. Blue Cross paid the whole $5,667.00 bill or around that. What a relief. Next I've joined the Perinton Chorus to sing the "Messiah." Ambulance training is going OK. Hopefully I'll soon be able to work it myself.

November 30, 1978

Observation LJE: True friendship dies hard, slow, intimacy yielding to indifference which breeds contempt. An eroding process—the river refusing to bend, cuts through the shore, a mound of grain dispersed by the wind grows ever smaller with each hour. Feelings harden, cold stones and dead fires on comfortless nights, made black, not by absence of stars or moon, but by self-pity, rejection. Unseen, yet permanent, these scars shape our lives. Believe it!

So what was so bad??? I broke up with Sue. After seven and a half months of knowing each other I did it. Why? It's hard to put my finger on. Perhaps I felt she was too good for me. She made me feel ashamed and selfish for wanting to have time to myself and for others. She hardly tried to make it this way. It was purely just a feeling I had. A silly one at that but Pat said something last night which settled it for me. What about 6 months from now? How will you feel with the decision you make today then? This hurts a lot more now but I hope in six months the pain will have passed. On the other hand, if this relationship continues as it has, I will surely be miserable in six months yet it would make the present more pleasant.

I backed out on our trip up to Toronto. Sue was very hurt and frustrated. She wanted to know what happened and I honestly couldn't say except that what we had is dieing and is close to being unsalvageable. Seems unfair that so much love should just pass by the wayside. It hurts very much though I mustn't let it show. I can be strong. I must fill myself with hope for tomorrow for the sun will shine. I will be alive. I will love again.

CLOSURE

Though these lips cry out in final
Farewell, my heart will not listen.
It is but an echo of pride
This "I don't care if you don't care"
Image.
Those first gentle feelings went
Unnoticed then what was it, merely a
Look, a glance that brought love's
Soft smile to life?
Now we pretend, we say it's
Over. We'll go away but what we
Felt not so long ago still remains as
Gossamer memories undisturbed
In the windless corners of our minds.

Chapter Eighteen

Homosexuality

"MY TURN"

No one that I've ever known
Cares the way you care.
I'd like to say I love you
But I know I wouldn't dare.

People just don't understand
And it makes me really mad.
Tell me how can love be wrong
How can it be bad?

Love and sex are not the same,
When will people learn?
When will love come my way,
Will I ever get my turn? LJE

Homosexuality

The question of your sexuality fluttered around in my mind like a butterfly in the breeze. It was neither heavy nor light...just a thought without judgment, without substance, certainly not a life-or-death issue. What is the history of homosexuality? It appears to have been with man since the beginning of time—an abnormality. Man is no different from other animals that shun or destroy the individual that is *different*. You felt that exclusion long before you knew. Do we send out messages in our aura? Children are so perceptive.

I ponder over your total rejection of your own feelings, your own sense of horror. You were so strong in so many ways, so forgiving, always reaching out to those in need, always trying to understand. Why couldn't you do for yourself what you did so freely and passionately for others?

The Summer with Suzanne, 1978

Maybe it was us? Were we unwittingly adding to your rejection of yourself? It wasn't that we didn't want you to have a close friend, LJ. We just didn't quite understand how you could be out day and night with Suzanne when she was married. Didn't she have to get dinner and do all those chores that I just took for granted? What kind of man would allow her continued absence? These are the things I asked myself, probably not wanting to ask the obvious question. How naïve. By the end of the summer, we were suspecting a sexual liaison. Did it shock us? It is obvious that it shocked and distressed you far more than us, for in those days homosexuality was still very much *in the closet*.

December 30, 1978

After the suicide attempt, which was caused mainly due to a physical attraction, I began feeling for her (Sue) and [having] fears of lesbianism, we drifted apart. For some time I saw a shrink ($60 for 45 min) but it didn't help much.

I suppose mainly through a maturing time I began to see things more clearly and to realize love should never be cast aside as if it never was so we are back together, emotionally speaking. We still care for and love each other in a healthier way. It is only too bad I still feel it must be kept from my parents. Maybe someday I can explain to them that I'm proud of my choice to admit to myself what happened and live with it and to live with myself.

We never spoke of your sexuality, LJ. That was between you and your doctors. Today, almost twenty-five years later, homosexuality is more out in the open. Accepted? Discrimination? Don't ask, don't tell? Same sex marriages? Today's political campaigns are still won or lost on people's acceptance or condemnation of gay marriages, but progress is being made. Ellen DeGeneres, an openly gay actress, is about the age you would be, fifty plus. She has starred in her own television show, MC'd an Oscar presentation, her face has been on many magazines. You could not fathom such acceptance. You were your own judge and jury. One of your heroines in life, Billy Jean King, is now living her life openly with her woman friend. These women all lived in your era, LJ. They accepted their predisposition—but you? There had to be something else!

When did the question of your sexuality arise? You had been without close girl friends in high school but that began to change. The first one I remember was Stephanie, when you were a teenager playing the Eastern tennis circuit. Stephanie invited you to Lyford Cay. Your remark to me, "Ma, I've been to a place you will never see. The wealth..."

Your description reminded me of *The Great Gatsby* with the fountains and the servants. The wealth. Did you envy it? Were you overwhelmed by it? Why the sadness I sensed when you returned? I believe it was there that you first expressed your feelings of love to Stephanie and frightened her and yourself. How old? Seventeen.

I go through your box, LJ, read the letters, the notes you made to yourself—the notice that you passed the fireman's written exam, the physical part with all the hoses was easy for you, you were so strong; the accounting of expenses and expenditures—but mostly there are the letters from women: Dottie, Sharon, Pat, Karen, so many women in your life that you loved and who loved you.

The following letter from Dottie, who you met in Cortland, may best describe your relationships that developed around the descending darkness:

Dear LJ,

I want you to know how much I care for you—the you that is bubbly and happy and smiles and sings and can be sad. I love that about. You make me so happy.

I don't even want to go back to school because it will hurt so much because you aren't there. I'm crying because of it, LJ. I was so content and confident around you. Even when you were depressed, you were still thoughtful and caring. I have to be honest with you though. As I have tried to be throughout our friendship. I am angry with the you that kept stringing me along with leading comments like "I'm going to miss you..." and torturing me by telling me about the gun and driving and your hose.

You never knew how much I was upset by it all. Now I'm mad about it. You couldn't accept that I love you and had to keep testing me to see just how much I could take. How far were you going to drag me before you would believe that you are good enough for someone to really love you? You can get mad at me for this and say "I'll show you," but the person it will hurt is you. I intend to write to you a lot and I hope to hear from you too but only from the LJ that wants to live!! Life is beautiful—you know it or you wouldn't be alive today. I know you can drive away the other part of you and I'm on your side. I will no longer tolerate the part of you that wants to die! Write to me, speak of how you feel, share your thoughts with me as we have in the past, just don't tell me of your death plans. I don't want to hear it.
Love, Dot

(for Dottie—a song someday)

I thank you for the smile my friend
The joy, the warmth and more
For love I feel will never end,
For opened hearts and doors.
I thank you for the warmth of spring
Your gentle way and touch,
For eyes that dance with joy and sing
Of dreams that mean so much.

Morrow you may be far away
But now you're here with me
So let us share the sun and day
As it was meant to be.
Thank you for your fortitude
It surely means a lot
For when I'm down you pull me thru
You're the best that I've got.
You've made the darkness yield to light
And set my spirit free.
The end has come to this long night
Leaving love and you and me.

Women have a special relationship, LJ. They bond in a different manner than men. It is a love, an understanding, a sharing. Little girls and their *best friends* are all a part of growing up that you did not experience, nor I. I believe you sensed that in me. "Ma, you never share yourself with anyone."

You were right. There was never any giggling, holding hands, running off to hide beneath the big willow tree with its lacy skirts shielding you from the world. I watch movies or my friends and hear their excitement, their squeals of delight. I do not believe there is a *squeal* in me, now or ever. I have always been on the edge of the abyss of emotions. A flat liner? I wonder, and sometimes feel cheated. I skirt the edges, never sharing or receiving the secrets of the heart. I've accepted that about myself, that I'm a Venutian from Mars (Dr. John Gray, *Men Are from Mars Women from Venus*) who needs her cave, but I do envy that close bonding.

Women rally around each other in a time of crises, circle the wagon so to speak. I learned throughout your journey that my friends were close by, not intruding, but standing strong. I have also had the friendship of your father—we are, indeed, best friends. I am blessed.

But you needed to be included in that inner circle. In your reaching out, you stepped over the boundary into what? The thrilling/horror of a physical love? As in *Phantom of the Opera,* you were drawn into the darkness of the night in you. You needed more. A need that developed or were you born to it? The years and denial dragged you down into the blackest of pits. Melodramatic? That was the fascination for you.

Chapter Nineteen

Sex in the City

In the forties and fifties, when we were growing up, *pregnant* was a whispered word, for you knew what that person had been doing! *Masturbation*? Yee gads, you knew you'd go blind if you practiced that! And so when my neighbor graduated—a good thing that gown was full—she had a "cyst" on her womb that was growing, which they ultimately named, John. We all knew she was pregnant, a ruined woman. By the way, that couple is still married after fifty plus years.

How did we, as parents, handle it, this sex thing? Not great, I guess, but I can't remember it being an issue. If you asked, I thought I answered your questions as candidly as I could. As non-church goers, you were never indoctrinated by the church fathers as to the *sin* of sex…guilt was not a *poison pill* of control. I believe each generation of parents does the best they can, and as we know, the raging hormones will not be denied.

You knew it and felt it long before you had a word for it…this sex thing. I think back to when you children started playing *doctor.* Children are upside down examining themselves practically before they can talk. That's how they learn. The trick for a parent is to make it seem natural, at the same time telling your children they can't do *that* in public.

What time is the appropriate time to have *The* talk? I believe your brothers and their wives are more aware and communicate more easily with their children, not only about sex, but in other aspects of responsibility. With today's explicit sex in the movies, on the computer, and in the school halls, plus the open controversy of gay marriages in the daily news, parents can hardly skirt the issue. Your father, who is presently involved in substitute teaching in the high school, speaks of overhearing two young girls talking about *yeast infections, contraception, and abortion.* Homosexuality is no longer a forbidden topic, and although it certainly is not totally accepted, it is tolerated in today's world.

I talk about today's mores with Sammy Sue, Kurt's fifteen year old. She ponders before telling me how many girls are virgins in her circle of friends. She then continues describing her group: "Well, one is a whore, and..." she clicks off their names.

It all seems so casual these days, this *sex* thing. I do not intrude into her own secrets, but we worry. I tell her frankly that masturbation (the new term is *solo sex)* is the only truly *safe* sex. Shocking? Probably, considering the teachings of almost every branch of religion—the dire warnings of *blindness, impotence,* and *insanity* which were the church warnings in our day are probably not outwardly taught today, but *sin* is still very much implied. I think most of the younger generation reject these teachings and will have little to do with religious hypocrisy considering the obscene actions of some of the church fathers. The world is indeed changing!

Today we worry about the killer AIDS and know that the billions of dollars spent by past president Bush's *Abstinence Only* program was/is ineffective. Sarah Palin's (vice presidential nominee in a past election) daughter was testimony to that. Understandably we hover over your nieces and nephews who teeter on the edge of adulthood and hold our breath as they face the same issues we faced, but in a high-tech world.

Would today's more honest and open attitude toward the gay community have been the answer to your dilemma? Questions unanswered. As I journey into the twenty-first century, I try to understand the changes but the *old ways* cling to me like my withered skin that no longer fits.

Romance

It all seemed so normal in those early years, the life we created. That summer when you were fifteen and Pierre was on the scene was a young girl's dream. This handsome Frenchman had eyes only for you, played tennis solely with you to the envy of all the other girls at the club. He took you to the movies and out for dinner (we advised you not to order "surf and turf.") He was nineteen and aware of your years. When he came back when you were seventeen, there were expectations that you rejected. Should we have taken note?

Then there was Roger, the young man you met working at Wegmans. How long was your relationship with him?

Was it truly your sexuality that was at the root of your problem? It is evident from your journals and letters in your chest that there were other would-be suitors. We never had the privilege of meeting Gregg whom you met in college or any of the other boys you dated.

desert studios

LJ

I'll have to say knowing you has been one of the best things that has ever happened to me. Just a few weeks ago I thought of how lucky I was to have met you and now it's time to say good-bye.

You came into my life and now you're leaving. But knowing you for the short time as I have has made my life a better one; now and forever. I guess in this last week I haven't cried so much since I was a little kid. As in the words of one of Chicago's songs....

....."*if you leave me now, you'll take away the biggest part of me.*"

Too true, but I guess that's the way it was supposed to be. I hope to see you often again someday. Until then, I'll be thinking of you always.

I love you
To Gregg:

BROKEN PROMISES

Whenever the dogs go crazy
I think maybe it's your face at the door,
Yet it's only night shadows dancing
Beneath a rising moon.
Memory dims, love fades
Even as the rose, and what
I felt briefly yet so strong
Is lost for eternity.
You said you were coming
Then never came. Now,
Even if you do
It won't be the same. LJE

Somewhere along the way, in the years of your incarceration (hospitalization without your consent), you met Frank. Engaged? How could that be?

Hi Lj

. had to fite you this letter I did not want you to think that ⊥ for got about you but I gess thats what you want me to do well ⁀ can not seem to do that so ⊥ hope that you do not mind that I rite to you. ⊥ hope that your holladays went but most of all ⊥ hope that you are doing good i think about you alot and i gess ¡ still hope that you will stop by and see me I gess ¸ nead to get it through my head that you will probley not do that. ¡ hope that you do not think that I am mad at you or wood not be here for you if you neaded me granted it made me feel preatty bad to have that happen but I can understand the reasons for whay you did it that way ⁀ was not giving you much of anything I am positive you cood find some one better to give you the things you nead and you will be happy. ⊥ only hope that you do not hate me or anything like that and I am truley sorey if I caused you any truble. ⊥ miss you alot and ⊥ still hope that mabe some day you will want to be friends againe. ⊥ am working hard on making my life better so that I will desyirve friends like you and Kath but lousing bough of you in the same twenty four hour made me realize how fucked up ⊥ was. ¸ wood like to do something to make up for messing up so bad with you. Please rember that I am here for you if ever you nead me.
take care of yourself I love you verry much ⸁rank

Frank. Where exactly did you meet Frank? Was it when you were in R-Wing at Strong? At the Institute of Living? Why weren't we ecstatic when you called and told us you were engaged? Was that before you told us that he was blind, that he had no family and was *working through* his problems? You told us not to worry, that you'd take care of him. Was that before your apartment was robbed and Frank disappeared (for a while)? Were we too cynical?

You asked why we couldn't just celebrate your love and wish you well. Oh, LJ, parents are much too protective and realistic to bless such a union. We see too far down the road and know what hardships lay in wait. Call them challenges if you like.

You had so many problems of your own. We knew that it took almost all of your energy to just get through the day at times. Where were you going to find the energy to take on the burden of Frank's problems? Of course, we wanted you to find love—that is what our journey here is all about—but we also knew the pitfalls of the wrong partner. Was there a way for us to be more positive? I know that we did not then, nor now have the wisdom of addressing these emotional volcanoes in ourselves, let alone in others. I'm sure Frank was there for you when you needed him, when you were raw with the ravages of your battles. How could you not love him for that?

Chapter Twenty

The call from Dr. Sobel informing us that you were so ill that either we commit you or she would no longer be able to treat you led to that first commitment to R-Wing at Strong Memorial Hospital. We tried to tell her that your first reaction would be to get out, that you would not allow anyone to dictate to you, that you had to be in control. We were so emphatic that she finally said impatiently, "They don't get out of R-Wing!" The underlying message, the first of many from the medical profession, was: What did we know? We were only your parents, and the suggestion was also–*the cause.*

We signed the papers at 9 AM; you were out by 11 AM.

"What is LauraJo doing out there?" A nurse asked.

You were sitting on the bench outside. One might have thought that would send a message to them–wrong. They brought you back in and you were gone again by 1 PM. It wasn't until about 4 PM that we got the call from Dr. Sobel: *Did we think she should call the police?*

Our question: "You told us our daughter was so ill that you wouldn't treat her unless we committed her. She's been out for over three hours and you are just now thinking about calling the police?"

The second call came about an hour later—you had been shot by the police and were in the hospital. He was young, the officer who shot you. He had been called on the job because of your call, the one where you informed the police that there was a woman in the parking lot of the hospital with a gun. In the few hours that you were out, you had purchased a starting pistol from a sports shop.

His gun was loaded with buckshot; his aim was the head. I mourned the loss of your eye, and then I closed both eyes and gave thanks. You wrote that officer a note of apology and never again, in all of your attempts, did you involve another person in your death wish.

The hospital's and Dr. Sobel's reaction? We heard nothing from them or the police department. No explanation. When the doctors told us your eye would have to be removed to prevent total blindness (a sympathetic reaction from the other eye), our anger grew. I called the head administrator of the hospital and threatened legal action. A meeting was set up with Dr. Harouotun Babigian, head of the Psychiatric Department. When we arrived, he picked up a large minute timer (similar to those used in the kitchen) and turned the knob. "You have fifteen minutes!" The ticking echoed.

Years later, when we investigated the possibility of legal action, you talked with the lawyers and your decision was not to pursue it, even though you were told you had a good case. The reason?

"It will ruin that nurse's career, Ma. I promised her I wouldn't run away when she took me for a walk."

We never spoke of the incident or the loss of your eye. You adjusted to your limited vision.

December 1978

To get down to resolutions…

1. Get down to 126 lbs by 6/20/79 from 158 lbs
2. Quit biting my nails
3. Quit picking my face

4. *Quit hurting myself when I'm mad or frustrated*
5. *Keep my goals ever in my mind and pray to God for guidance and help*

Some of this year's "firsts" were: (Age 21)
1. *My first high (pot) 5/78*
2. *My first drunk 6/19/78*
3. *My first "in bed" which was awful. I did it only to find out
   what it was like and it hurt like hell!*
4. *My first minimum wage job (Wegmans cheese shop)*
5. *My first genuine suicide attempt…Oct 2, 1978*

*1978 also held 4 trips to the emergency room for: sniff-
ing Pam cooking spray, taking a bottle of tranquilizers with
wine. Taking a bottle of nodoze and my carbon monoxide poisoning, which meant 5 days in intensive care and 2
weeks in R-Wing which came to $5,6887 or around that.
My insurance covered it. Thank God.*

*My relationship with Mom and Dad went up and down this
year more than average. We had our disagreements. All in
all, it was a year in which I really grew up a lot. I'm learning
how to better cope with my depressions and frustrations. It
was a year where love came to me in bounty, forgiveness
and patience alike.*

*It is a year to thank God for, to thank friends and family for,
to be grateful for merely surviving. I only hope 1979 is a bit
more uneventful.*

Chapter Twenty-one

February 1979

Christmas was fantastic even though it was just the four of us…Mom, Dad, me, and Kurt. Mom made the traditional buffet table with lots of homemade cookies. She did all the baking this year because my two part time jobs kept me very busy. I played my guitar and we all sang. I'm getting less shy about it all the time. Mom read from the bible then we proceeded to open our presents. We woke up Christmas morning to 1 ½ inches of snow. Surprise! So, of course, we went skiing. First time of the year. Ma stayed home.

January came and the new year, but not without some changes. The first man came into my life. Roger: 24, blond, cute and ever so nice. We hit it off from the start and I have to say I kicked the whole thing off by talking to him in Wegmans and setting up a paddle game. After that, it seemed the snowball was rolling.

We have a lot in common. We love sports and a good time, we love each other's company and who knows maybe someday we'll love each other. Roger helped speed January along. Friday nights were spent w/Sue. We are still friends. Not as close but it is better, I think.... With the end of January came the start of school (Cortland) and the death of my car! Then the next weekend I went home or rather to his place. We haven't had sex though we've slept together. I'm just not ready. I don't know what's wrong with me. He just can't turn me on. Maybe I'm frigid. Ha. I hope not.

February 14, 1979

Today was Valentine's day. I got three. One from my mom and dad, one from Roger and one from poor old Sue. I was kind of hoping for a flower but they're expensive. Emotionally I'm O.K. Do think bad thoughts not actions. Going strong and hanging on. Over and out LJ.

March 4, 1979

Observation LJE: To become wise, one must not separate oneself from pain.

No one in the world is home today. I've tried them all, Roger, Sue, Carrie, Mom and Dad…I'm so sad today. A controlled sorrow, that being its only good point! I hate school, the pressure, the senseless work. It depresses me. I'm a sluff. I want life to be easy. To be fun. Or am I kidding myself, would I get bored? Oh hell, I can't say anything for certain anymore, except I need something now, I need someone to dry my tears and someone to explain to me why the tears?

Happiness, I know, is not a place but a state of mind. My mind is not in that state. All I…what will do the trick? Can Roger? Sue can't, Mom and Dad try. God won't or at least hasn't.

I'm so pent up right now I don't want to do anything but sit and stew. I don't want to study, to go to the movie, to play my guitar. I could really get off on eating but refuse to. I was awful last night, cookies, a sundae, cheese burger… sickening!

I wish Roger were here. I've called and called. He's not home. Thank Heaven he didn't get the job in Iowa. I'd hate to lose him. I'm really starting to love him; I think and that's saying a lot. I've never loved a man except Dad & Jeff & Kurt but of course that's different. I wonder what those two boys are up to anyway.

*God anything is making me cry today------------
HEEELLLLPPP me out of this mess someone. I'm screw-
ing up something awful. It's there again tonight, stronger
than I've felt it since I left the hospital, the frustration, the
anger, the confusion, the constant thought of how will I try
it this time? Will I end up back in R-wing? Will I go to "hell"?
Dammit! Stop it! Call someone, no, no I don't need to. It
won't help. It never does. Just writing this seems to help a
little. I won't conform. I won't "succeed." For them I want to
or maybe because of them I don't want to. What's wrong,
LauraJo? Why can't you just live?*

April 2, 1979

*March is gone and April has arrived. At times I wonder If
I'll see May.*

*My week in Florida was fair. Roger and I didn't hit it off
real well. It was my fault. I was dull and didn't want to do
many of the things he wanted to do. A lot of the things he
said and did bothered me for no real reason. I didn't want
to neck or kiss or anything that I'm supposed to want to do
and according to Roger I never will want to if I don't want
to now. Tough shit. If all men want is to fuck around, they
can do it w/a cow till they die of a heart attack (the guy not
the cow). Sex seems to be the most important thing in the
world to most men. They can have it. I know it's impt. to
lots of women too but that doesn't affect me.*

**Observation LJE: To interpret what is unclear, is
to create new uncertainty.**

*People say they want to understand, to help, but they can't
if they can only see things by their standards and priorities;*

and how can one change these things and who's to say they should. Our problems are our own, to be worked out, as in solitaire. People can share your love, your joy, these they can get into but sorrow and pain...who but a fool would not turn from these. Each of us has enough of this to cope w/on our own, right?

I think of how sorry I may be, of how I may go to "hell," of how I owe everyone more than this but then I think about their freedom of choice and how they did what they wanted. We shared. All I have loved have taken a part of me for their own, and given a part in return.

Observation LJE: Patience is like a rubber band. If worn to a breaking point, it lashes out hurtfully at that which sorely tested it. Forgive me for stretching you that far.

I wonder if I'm really concerned w/the temporary hurt they will feel or if I want them to feel it. I can't see any reason for this. I believe I would spare them if I could but I can't live my life for others. I can only live for myself and share this w/others. If I take what is only mine and God's to take, it shouldn't be a personal insult to anyone.

My love for my family & friends goes deep, though the question will most certainly be asked why wasn't their love alone enough to make me happy, to make me want to live. There are too many other things. Real or imagined, I'm not certain. Perhaps if I'd only waited, been more patient but it's been four years now. Four years of saying, "At last it's over. I can go on w/my life now."

But to say it started 4 yrs ago is not altogether true. There were things before that even when I was a child I had dreams of being shot and sometimes killed. Not just occasional dreams but extremely frequent. The same dreams bringing injury and death by night and when I got older and occasionally went swimming, I would blow out all my air and sink to the bottom of the pool lifelessly imagining I was dead and then in later dreams through high school I became suicidal (only in the dreams) I was suicidal for a night in my dreams and it shocked me. I couldn't understand when I woke up how I could ever dream such an awful thing. I couldn't believe I would ever feel that way. Then after high school into college it got worse. I started hurting myself when the frustration became unbearable, hitting my head on walls, punching myself in the face, taking bottles of aspirin, going w/out water for days, fasting, speeding around crazily on my motorcycle, climbing cliffs w/out ropes. It came in waves like a pulsing force driving me to do dangerous things. The pendulum swung from relative happiness to extreme sorrow w/out an observable reason. I didn't even know what triggered it.

So many people tried to help. First there was Sharon, then Carrie then Suzanne and now Dottie. They all were willing to give me 110%. More than anyone could ask for or should need but it didn't matter. I could be sitting right next to anyone of them and feel so totally alone. What was it I needed? What unattainable part of me is missing that no one can help me find? God bless them for trying, and if it is at all possible, help them to at least try to understand and perhaps forgive me, but if the only thing that will stop the pain is for them to hate and curse me then I will take it. I don't want to hurt them. I just want the pain to stop, the hopelessness to end. They can call me a quitter, a fool. Perhaps they are right. If it is possible, I'll probably regret it but this time is it! No more false alarms or high hospital bills. Just one small cremation and a simple I'm sorry to disappoint you all and I'm sorry to myself for quitting.

I don't deserve any last requests but if you wouldn't mind, I'd like to give my car to Dottie. She's kind of poor and will never be able to afford a car like mine or at least for a long time. Anyway, I'm sure you won't want it around & if Dottie doesn't want it, just sell it. Mom, I love you. I'm a part of you and you are a part of me. We have shared so much and I'll never regret our closeness.

Dad, it took me a long time to realize how special you are. Besides Jeff and Kurt, you are one of the few men I can truly say I love. Don't take this personally, please. I love you more than you can know. Please forgive me and go on w/your life.

For Dad

26 years you've been my dad
    And yet thru all those days
I never quite saw you clearly
    Only thru a childs haze.

Scholar, lover, and scientist,
    A quiet gentle man
I've grown to love you more each day
    And now I understand...

You gave me all you had to give,
    More than I'll ever know
I feel abundantly grateful
    And want to let it show
You've been a wonderful father
    The best that there could be
and now I want to give to you
    The love I feel in me.
It's not too late, We're both still young,
    We've yet so much to do.
I've gotten to know me better
    Now I'd like to get to know you.

A poem for pop

Lotsa Love

Laurajo

Everything's going fine

Jeff, you're a prize among men. I love your sincerity and dedication in all that you do. It will take you to the top. Be strong thru the hard times. They will not last.

Kurt, the man of action and bad breaks when it comes to knees. My love for you is woven w/memories of make-believe and tickling fights. You were always such an observant young man, taking in nature's beauty w/an unreserved eye. Your imagination spun wild tales and your smile was free to all. May your carefree attitude last and keep you strong in the face of the future burdens.

Granny, we've had our ups and downs. I admire your ability to change w/the times and roll w/the punches. You're very special. Thank you for all you've given me. I can give only my love in return.

Sharon gave me love & the ability to touch & be touched. Carrie gave me a song and a flower and a sunset. But mostly the ability to laugh & sing. Suzanne gave me patience, understanding and an undying love. She stuck w/ me thru it all and I love her for loving me so much.

Dottie has cared and loved me so much in the little bit of time I've known her. I hope she has many special people in her life to share her abundant love and happiness. She's as bubbly as spring and I love her as much as any of my longer acquainted friends & I hope she bounces back fast.

I've got it planned to prevent any chickening out this time. I'm going to get so stoned I pass out then I can't get out. I can't change my mind and blow it again. I left out Roger. The one other man in my life. Patient, caring, full of energy and good deeds. I believe if I weren't so disturbed I would realize how very perfect he is and accept him if he'd have me. I can't do it. I can't let him have me, hug me, or kiss me even. Before I could but I'm getting worse. I don't even want to think of men and how I'm supposed to feel for them. I hate it.

There's not much else to say. Only that I've really tried. I went to the damn shrinks, the school counselors. Did it help? No! I did try. What can I say? Except go on, live, do what I failed and don't feel sorry for me. I had it & blew it. Hate me if you have to. Do anything to ease the pain. I love you all always. Love never dies. LauraJo

Observation LJE: The years of my affliction have become a long and mournful echo not fit for any ear.

My mind is racing. I don't know what I'll do. I've already bought a garden hose. I'm afraid. I'm afraid this time I'll really go away and it won't be good. It won't rid me of the anguish I feel. It will double, but still I'm inclined to try. I want to call someone, Mom or Dad, Pat or Char. I want to be stopped but I won't give them the chance. I've drug too many people down, put so many whom I love thru so much. They must tire of it and in all fairness I can't do it anymore. I won't. This will be the final blow then they can all breathe a sigh of relief and go on w/their lives. My guilt is strong, my apologies many, my fear great.

This is the only path left to me. I promised myself not anyone else that I would die before I dropped out again. If only the end to it all were in sight then maybe I could hang on, but it goes on and on and I can't.

Chapter Twenty-two

April 8, 1979

Well look who's here. Me! Surprised? Pleased? Don't know. Dr. Jekyll is still winning out over Mr. Hyde.

It is on my mind constantly even when I'm happy it lurks in the back of my mind, peeking from the shadows like some hideous beast. Oh how I hate it. Hate its prodding, it's dedication to my sorrow.

I used to believe that love could cure anything. Now I don't know....someone tell me, tell me please......I can't bear this much longer. I am outside myself looking down at a stranger. It is an odd feeling which comes and goes. I can't explain it, yet it is very odd...It's as if a part of me leaves for a moment and becomes a stranger looking on from outside my comprehension. That doesn't explain it. Maybe it's crazy, but it scares me. It makes me think something, someone, is waiting to take over my body. To perhaps appreciate it the way it should be appreciated. Yet I feel this thing is to blame. It is evil and is making me feel like I do in an effort to get me do myself in. It makes me believe that sadness and sorrow are an eternity that this anguish will never go away. No one can ever know what it's like. I want to kill it, to make it stop.

But there are no guarantees. Perhaps even after death it would be there. My hell for eternity. There is an insanity w/in me. I feel it clawing at my insides to get out. Perhaps it's just my own active imagination. I hope so. I hope I'm just making something out of nothing… words are so inadequate at times. There are no words for truth.

Truth is silent as the passage of time or the first rays of sunlight and no matter how fast I run, I can't catch truth… it eludes me. It laughs at me. It's not fair, I don't want to go yet, but the rules are clear…if you can't play by them you're out of the game. I just can't seem to make my own rules anymore and I can't play by theirs. I can't conform and I can't bear the loneliness of not conforming. So what's left?

April 11, 1979

Boy, am I getting sick of writing in this thing, but there's nothing else to do. I don't go to class, I don't study, I don't play my guitar, I don't even cry anymore. I just sort of hang around waiting, waiting to get up the nerve… People think I'm strong. Maybe I was four years ago, but I'm running out. My body's screaming "no!", it won't take it anymore. Enough is enough. Perhaps I shall never know what rips my insides out at regular intervals, what makes a quitter out of someone who would once fight her best at whatever she undertook. Where did she go? I wish people would get beyond the exterior. Obviously suicidal tendencies needn't have anything to do w/exterior happenings or surroundings. Sure, often times a lost love, or loneliness, but often there is none of this. There is love and wealth and opportunity, but no one can see inside. No one can see the invisible drive, the things that a person can convince themselves are true. Even if they are not true. The hopelessness a person can feel.

This poem I give to Carrie, to Sue, to Sharon, to Dottie, the outsiders who have come in to try to help. They gave me their love freely, the strength endlessly, and their patience faithfully. I will love them as my family always. I hope they realize how special they are to me even now.

You're on my mind, you and your gentle ways.
I struggle to see your face but I can't recall.
All I remember is your constant smile. More
Often a cover up, hiding fears and doubts.
I wish I could smooth out your troubles yet
First I must smooth my own. It takes time
To turn over a new leaf. Time and patience.
I wish it could happen overnight and in a
Way I suppose it does. Over many a night.
The gradual change surfaces like a lily on the
Face of a pond. A tender bloom fragile in its
Delicate beauty. I, like the flower, have my
Roots far below the surface of my exterior,
Therein lays my strength.

April 12, 1979

Today is the day. Tonight, the night. I can't face them w/ failure. I can't tell them I'm failing, that I can't or won't face my responsibility. I'm sick of quitting, sick of running and it doesn't seem anyone can help me, and oh how I want help. How many ways must I ask? How many times? "You've got to work harder at it," they say. Can't they see that's the prime symptom of the problem. The resignation of effort. Dammit I'm so tired of it all. There seems only one way to end it. One way to solve the problem and if it follows me after this, well then I just can't know...

April 13, 1979 (Strong R-Wing)

DAMN – I fucked it up again. They're all right. I'm not suicidal. The only really suicidal people are dead. Right??? God, Mom & Dad piss me off. They're so understanding, nice & helpful. They'd help me more if they just threw me out. If they'd just ignore me. It's worse here, and I hate to be negative but what's going to make this time any different from the rest...I've given up believing in magic.

Suicide Precautions! Ha. If they think that will stop me they've got another thing coming. I can outwit them...Pat nor Char are here tonight...Don't know if I want to see them...and Sobel...I don't know if we really communicate...Ma said I just haven't given her a chance. Well let me tell you at $1 a minute I'd like to see some results! I don't think that's too much to ask.

Now about ol Suzanne, who has completely forgot I'm alive. I hope she's just a little bit sorry when I'm gone. Not too much just a little. I truly do want everyone to bounce back. I'm sure they will, just like little rubber balls. Human nature is just that way, thank God. Here I sit in my little private room ($11 a day extra) plotting my next move. Will it be tonight, tomorrow, or who knows maybe I'll get cured. Fat chance. You're a quitter Laurajo, you Jack Ass. Ma says she's loved me all these years and I owe her. Didn't

I love her back? Didn't I give as much as I took. They had me not vise-versa.

April 15, 1979

Here it is Easter Sunday. Whopee-dooo. R-Wing is as wild as a graveyard on Saturday night.

I've decided for sure I don't want to work with Sobel. We don't relate...Pat came in and told me she was my nurse for the day...the only one I want to see again...I can talk to her....she's only here one day a week...I need more than that....does it matter? I'm ready to leave right now... where...does it matter...will it change things? Maybe, I think not. Do I care? Sure I want to fix this mess but I can't be caged, I won't be. I'd rather die than be locked up... Sobel says I'm afraid of shrinks...I'm not afraid of anything except life sometimes. I guess I'm not crazy about pain either or loneliness. I like singing & laughing and being with my friends when I'm happy because they can be happy too. I don't want to see my parents. Maybe ever again. I'm not sure why. Perhaps I hate them for my own shortcomings and their generosity. That sounds fair doesn't it? I've either got to do it or quit it. I'm sick of these places. Yuck!

God help me! Hey God, I hear from Welton down here that you're a man. Well if that's the case, stick it! I don't want anything to do with you. But I don't believe that is the case so please help me out. I don't think I'm asking for a miracle am I? Well, even so...you kept me alive and whole through all this shit, what's one little gift of peace-of-mind? Please. I'll work for it. I'll try but don't let me down, God. I'm tired of the hurt, the dead end turns. There's got to be a way out. Just point. I'll go...even if it's all up hill. Come on. I'm ready. I just hope you are.

May 24, 1979, 10:00 PM

Observation LJE: You told me you'd be there. Now I look and you're nowhere to be seen. Was it a trick to amuse me or idly please me? If so, I'm not pleased but saddened.

Loneliness like a cold wind lurks in every niche of my mind. A haunting presence so easily stirred to reality I cannot ignore its existence. I used to believe love ruled the universe, that it could cure all ills, yet I have so very much love, far more than my share and still I search, search for a substance which will fill the emptiness within me. Such a fathomless void subject to no rule of rhyme or reason, it abides in pressing sadness always upon me. What good is a world where nothing matters, where not even love is enough anymore? My search goes on, a journey without end. Like a rainbow, but lacking the beauty, it stretches before me, from yesterday thru today on beyond tomorrow. The hope is gone. So often it just seems impossible to be optimistic, to look beyond today to tomorrow. How sad to be so negative at such a young age and with so very many talents. Why God? Why give me talents yet no ability to enjoy them. Shit that really stinks. They'll say I was a quitter, a coward and perhaps I am but I can't go on like this. There's just too much pain, too much emptiness. When will it end? Must I die to find peace? Must I throw away all my treasures of friends and talents and health?

Observation LJE: As a runner nearing the finish, I fear an end and a new beginning.

How far must I run to escape myself? The answer is obvious to a blind man yet I keep running, keep trying. If it can be done, I'll do it. That is one thing that is certain.

I look at the date of this entry: May 24, 1979 and I anguish over the duration of your struggles, LJ. Years, with no more than slight momentary relief and I shake my fist at your God!

Chapter Twenty-three

June 3, 1979

It is difficult for me to think positive. It's almost as if death has become an obsession with me, a challenge to be met and conquered. Why the difficulties? It should be easy. Let's see, there's pills…nope, I barf every time. I've tried cooking spray…no luck, glue…nope, fasting 14 days…too slow-gave up, heat & cold extremes…not long enough. Is there any way to end the loneliness? How can I be freed from the burden w/in me? Where is the answer? There is so little to gain and so much to lose by it all, and yet I go on hurting myself as if it were a duty. Where can I run to; where can I hide from this raging tide, this force w/in me. There is no place far enough away and besides I don't want to die in a strange place all alone!

June 24, 1979

I guess I could say a lot has happened since my last entry in this book…Let's just say I let it build up again to the boiling point…So here I am back in R-Wing with 24/ hr nurses….I wait to go to Hartford and the Institute of

Living. I heard it's pretty good…at the price it ought to be! I hope it works out! Sometimes I feel like it's my last hope.

Institute of Living: July 2, 1979, through May 30, 1980 (first stay)

The Institute of Living in Hartford, Connecticut, was highly recommended to us by the doctors at the University of Rochester, and by Dr. Joan Sobel. There were four of us that made that first trip to Connecticut. We asked Jeff to come with us to help with any unexpected emergencies. We knew you were in a desperate mood. As a precaution we removed the door handle and had Jeff sit next to you in fear that you'd leap from the car. The chaos of what must have churned through your mind could only be imagined. To commit you against your will—would it be like the commitment to Strong? We were hopeful that this would be different, that by this time you would understand the need.

July 2, 1979

They picked me up at 5:30, on time for a change. I survived the drive and arrived on time with a rigged car door on one side and Dad or Jeff on the other. Ma would go with me to the bathroom and Jeff would wait outside. I bet they thought it was a job well done. Their precious but "sick" daughter had been delivered to her place of salvation in one piece, so I read my rights, signed some papers and talked with two shrinks for about half an hour. Then we went thru the secret tunnels which keep the secure sectioned off with a multitude of locked doors which eventually led to my "maximum security cell" with a lot of very sick inhabitants. They jerk, they shake, they stare into space and talk to imaginary people. They scream and cry and laugh at nothing. For fun they smoke, knit, and do a lot of sitting around. Unlike Strong Memorial this place w/its astronomical fee has extra charges for all activities, and necessities such as soap, envelopes, and anything besides the three meals a day, a bed and with some time with a shrink. WOW, what a great deal. The staff seems nice enough but boy did I get a scare today...I saw this black switch which buzzed when I hit it. About a doz. staff came running down the hall full speed. I guess it was an emergency switch!

The only outdoors I'll see is a 30 ft. square courtyard w/12 ft. high walls. There is zilch to do...only one sitting room with one TV and one radio...everyone chain smokes... It's really the pits. I did come hoping for an environment where I'd have the freedom to develop and work on some constructive self help...

There is absolutely no freedom. Every door is locked, every window opaque, every room closet size and dirty w/one tiny window in the wall and an even tinier one in the door. There are the standard seclusion rooms and a couple bathrooms. Everything is extra like I said, including laundry soap and the machines. I'm surprised the showers and johns are not coin operated. The little store has way overpriced stuff which one can sign for and there is one phone which hooks up to a switch board.

It's really the pits. I decided to sign myself out. I don't ever want to see or talk to my mom again. They're claiming my tape deck...their hassling my friends...I hate them sometimes for making decisions about my life, for lying, saying I could do what I want now then having me locked up. That really sucks.

Someone is sobbing uncontrollably, someone is bragging about suicide, someone is swearing, someone is talking to their hallucinations, and someone is praising the Lord

w/an anxious heart. Where do I fit in w/all these people,
Lord? How could my parents do this to me? Oh help me,
fulfill my trust. Keep me strong...I myself no longer live,
but Christ lives in me...

> I see them, old and young
> Crazy and not, still, all depressing
> And I am part of this, part of the
> Craziness, the seclusion, the
> Side Room, the wet packs.
> I want to go away from it.
> Depart to the real world but
> Now this is my real world..

They never allowed us to see you in your *quarters* at the Institute of Living... always a visiting room. But from your journals, I get the picture of a modern-day snake pit—high windows for protection, from escape? People strapped in their chairs to keep them from tearing out their eyes, people so over drugged that their stares were vacant, walk, nothing more than a shuffle. We saw the same environment in R-Wing at Strong. What did we expect? Compared to the other patients you seemed so normal. We hated leaving you in that environment, hated the vague, diagnosis of *Disturbed.* For you it was all experimental, a *let's-try-this* approach.

Thus began the first months of an eleven-month stay in Hartford with Dr. W. Scarborough as your physician. When we asked Dr. Scarborough about his expertise, how he was assigned to you, what was his professional diagnosis, there was no answer. Was it a random assignment, darts at a dartboard? His silence echoed. It was as if we needed to establish some "need to know". His only response was a repetition of his dire warning, "We generally don't get patients as ill as LauraJo, we usually find them dead."

But they didn't know your strength and courage! Thus, we shielded ourselves, never accepting the possibility of the accuracy of their diagnosis.

Our visits, as allowed, were one-day affairs. We would get on the road by 4:30 AM; arrive in time to see the social worker and the doctor for approximately an hour. We must have talked about something, but certainly no information about your treatment (patient-doctor privilege). It was weeks before we received a diagnosis, *Borderline Personality,* an illness not recognized by many in the psychiatric profession. My research revealed a very sketchy description of an illness with symptoms that overlapped other known mental disorders. We received no outline of treatment, no description of proposed medication, no estimate of a recommended length of hospitalization.

July (contd.)

Observation LJE: Home calls to me like a sweet song on a summer's night. Memories, hopes and dreams meld into one. The child in me looks back in longing. Yet the years have swept me away. Lying on the shore, I drag myself up and am ready to move on.

Something came to me today, in thinking back about the flood I began to realize how it changed me. I used to save everything, now I have few possessions and don't want many. I used to just live without question, feel without wondering why I felt as I did but on that day it was as if my eyes were opened, my heart jumped into overtime and I became very sensitive to others besides my immediate family. In the movie, Earthquake--the tears, so much suffering! And I felt it all. It was as if it were happening to me.

I seemed to be flashing back to the flood. I wanted to give of myself to those I felt drawn to. I wanted to find me, LauraJo, connected, before it was too late, before a tidal wave swept through my life and took me away. It was after this, the brush with potential death, having had less than a minute to react, that I bought my first motorcycle, tried my first parachuting, wanted to hang glide, scuba dive. It was after this that I felt the anguish of saying the words "I love you" when for the first time I felt the need to hurt myself because I loved and was afraid of this love, afraid it would end and I'd be left all alone, afraid it would end suddenly and w/out warning stolen away by a "sleeper wave" in the night. Fear drove me to loneliness, which drove me to desperation.

Such emptiness, helpless, hopeless…I'd rather be dead. So often since that day I wondered why I had not been killed, torn away in a car that wouldn't start by a dark cold wall of water. I refused to believe that the loss of things could matter in the least. No lives had been lost. So what happened? Why was everything so magnified, so intense. Where did that girl who was so all-together go? Why even in looking back did everything look so bleak. Worst of all, I gave the blame to Mother. Sure our relationship had a lot to do with it but something happened after that flood that took my ability to cope away. And now I'm so afraid, afraid that I won't be able to ever cope again.

July 9, 1979, 4:20 PM

Three times a week for half an hour (doctor visits). *I wonder how long I'll be here with this intense amount of therapy. I did remember one thing though thinking back. When I was twelve, I dove off the head of a flight of stairs head first. I was sleepwalking and didn't wake up. Surely if I had been awake and tensed myself, I would have broken my neck. He asked me if I ever had severe headaches following this incident but the only thing I can recall (and I don't know if it was before or after) were times at night when I would try to go to sleep and my head would spin so violently that I would have to open my eyes and put my foot out onto the floor. Yet still every time I closed my eyes, the spinning returned and I would be afraid and cry. This would go on until I was so exhausted I would fall asleep.*

I only went to Mom and Dad once about it. In tears and exhaustion, I got up in the night and tiptoed to their room. I didn't know what to say except that I felt like I was turning "inside-out." Those are the words I could remember using, "Inside-out" and I couldn't make it stop. Sometimes it wouldn't even stop when I opened my eyes and that would scare me even more but always I would eventually fall asleep. I guess I was around 12 but like I said, I don't remember if it was before or after the sleepwalking fall.

Then he asked me about my vision and if I'd ever seen spots, or lights. I remember in Jr. high, I think it was 7th or 8th grade, that would make me around 13…I can remember being in gym class and my ears would start to buzz, then my vision would change. Wherever I looked I would see a bright light yet my peripheral vision was still OK so I would stand and look out of the corner of my eyes. It would last about 15 minutes then I'd be OK. I never told anyone. I just figured that maybe someday I'd need glasses and now I do (ha) for quite different reasons though. I don't know what it all means. I haven't thought back about it for ages because it doesn't happen anymore. I think it happened less than a dozen times anyway over a period of maybe 6 months.

July 16, 1979

Such rage, violent rage is masked beneath this calm carefree exterior. A disguise to fool even the keenest eye, even the inner eye. I sometimes fool myself, then there's an eruption and the anger spills forth in a fury frightening to behold, leaving in its wake a deceiving calm filled with more destruction than the rage itself was, yet this rage is turned silently inward toward self destruction. A relentless search for peace and rest though I feel at times not even death will calm this sea of turmoil.

July 18, 1979, 8:45 AM

These days pass with many free hours. I've time to think, to pray, to wonder just what I'm expected to acquire here. Wisdom? Understanding? Perhaps, but it comes not from an outside reservoir. It is drawn out from within, through leading questions, through quiet meditation and prayer. Through trust in God to be always with me. His eye ever on me. His ear ever harkening to my cry.

Through the hours here I am able to think more clearly, to envision a hopeful and positive future. I am able to reach out to God for support and strength, to trust Him and pray that I will be set free soon, hoping that the purpose of my being here is nearly accomplished. I will probably be on this low unit for my entire stay here, which ought not be more than 8 more weeks. I think it only a fair compromise that after giving my folks two months of a prison term, that they allow me to leave. I'll have done my time. I am the butterfly burst from the cocoon. Alive again, beautiful, a new creation. I am LauraJo, connected, sensitive, and caring, afraid and lonely at times. I'm impatient and head strong at times but I'm human, I laugh, I cry, I sing and dance. I live and love and want so much out of life. I want to do all that I do to my very best, to be all that I'm capable of. I watch life pass by me and strive to believe that it is necessary for me to be here at this time. Something good will come of it all. Praise the Lord.

Chapter Twenty-four

At the Institute, your therapy was left largely to your own doctoring through your writing, and meditating. But as Grandpa Joe advised…doctors don't cure: "I never cured anyone; I just held their hand until they cured themselves." The high price of the Institute of Living provided safety *for* you *from* you, and it bought relief for us. For the moment you were safe…we thought. How far did you get when you escaped?

Awareness. You hid your pain so well, but we could no longer deny the evidence of your illness. There were times when you were hardly recognizable; your head was so swollen from banging it against the wall. Later on, you spoke of being blind when your one good eye swelled shut. The razor blades, the beating of your arms and legs, the rat poison, the salt…all this for relief? Where did the pain come from?

I asked it then and today I still ask, *where did the pain come from*? Emotional pain is difficult to understand. In reading your journals, I am overwhelmed all these years later by your suffering and the medications you were subjected to throughout your treatment: Haldol, one of your greatest fears, along with Anafranil, Parnate, and others. Your complaints of effected eyesight, and hearing, your writing that became so small it was unreadable as if you were disappearing, the LJ we knew. The explosive anger, raging tantrums that were treated with wet packing. The months at the Institute dragged from July into the winter. Our trips were every two weeks. Sometimes we saw you and other times, at your request, we did not.

From your journals there are so many questions about life. Questions I never asked at your age. I just accepted my life the way it was and tried to deal with the daily happenings as best I could.

July 19, 1979

My peace faded a bit today but has returned w/the prayers of Pastor King and myself. Praise fills my soul and lies upon my lips. There is beauty within, light within, peace w/in. It goes beyond what even Judy can understand. For I believe that I will even be at peace with my mother again.

I am facing perhaps my last chance for a future. I must not run away this time. I must stand and face the dragon. Though I may be singed in battle, I must fight now before it is too late.

The days unfold, long
And tiresome in their boredom.
Rise, shower, eat, sit, sleep
Reclining in blank stares.
No smiles, no hope, you
Get lost in yourself, sinking
Beneath the half light
Between reality and depression.
"You're sick" they say. "We
Only want to help." How about
A little encouragement.
"No...don't want to give
False hope," or surface a smile!

Your beseeching was strongest during the early days of your stay at the Institute of Living, your hate for us for committing you against your will most vocal. Our trips became routine, only varying by weather dictates. Our life was in a state of limbo, like a picture paused between frames.

August 23, 1979. Thursday, 7:00 PM

Lots to catch up on today. For instance, I've been packed five times in the last four days. Sunday, Monday, Tuesday, and twice Wednesday. It was only on the fifth packing that I didn't fight like a hell-cat and they didn't need fourteen guys to hold me down, strip me, and tie the restraints. If anything in my life has ever made me feel like an animal CWP did, that's "cold wet packs," sheets soaked in cold water then wrapped around the problem (me) and restrained with a multitude of canvas restraints. Very restraining to say the least and very hot despite the name for it. As four out of the five times or rather five out of the six times I fought very hard in restraints but the sixth time I was just too exhausted. I felt beaten, depleted, empty. There just wasn't anything left. I'd lost. I was defeated.

Self-abuse

It wasn't until we visited you at the Institute of Living that your self abuse became evident even to us…a head so swollen we could barely recognize you from your head banging, wrists and other parts of your body bandaged from cutting and gouging.

Self-mutilation is something I could not understand. Dr. Kumetat tried to explain: "Imagine pain so severe that you would slam your hand in the car door for relief!"

Why didn't I see evidence of your self-abuse earlier? Was I blind? From your journals, I read the details and I shudder. Were your aggressive symptoms, never exhibited by you in the past, partly the results of an overload of chemicals? As noted, you were terrified of Haldol. (Haloperidol--an antipsychotic drug that had more adverse side effects than some of today's drugs, suicide being one of them.) It was on a trip home from the Institute that we overheard in a restaurant, "Don't ever prescribe Haldol, it's much too dangerous."

We understood that anger release was the goal. Try as you and the doctors would over the years, no method was found, no safe avenue of escape for the release of the anger that churned within you.

So were we wrong to refuse the **experimental** drug alternative from Dr. Scarborough at the Institute of Living—his dire warning repeated, and that cute little, boot-wearing social worker who asked us, "Why are you killing your daughter?"

All this from the psychiatric profession. Your father would have signed the papers; I would not. Your plea

> ☐ **Nearly half of US teens mutilate themselves.** Forty-six percent admit to cutting or burning their bodies...biting themselves...or picking at their skin to draw blood. Self-injury is glorified in some movies, songs and Web sites. Teens who do it say it gives them a sense of control over their lives...or that the physical pain distracts them from mental or emotional distress. *More information:* Go to Self-injury.com, or call 800-DONT-CUT.
>
> Elizabeth E. Lloyd-Richardson, PhD, assistant professor of psychiatry and human behavior, Brown Medical School and The Miriam Hospital, both in Providence, and leader of a survey of 633 high school students, published in *Psychological Medicine.*

echoed. If this drug (Haldol) that was FDA approved could be disastrous, what would *experimental* drugs be? And so we brought you home. After considering all of the alternatives we were offered, and knowing your disposition, we turned the control of your health care over to you. Right? Wrong?

Home from the Institute of Living...a week? Two weeks? Several months? You decided to go back. Another three months and you returned home and started looking for a new doctor. The next thing we knew you were tying ropes to the balcony.

Were you too sick to handle your own health care, to make a sane choice? We knew that if we committed you again to still another institution that all of your energy would be spent as it was at the Institute and Strong—to get out. How old were you? Twenty one/twenty two? What doctors were you seeing then? There had been so many—Freudian, chemical, psychologists.

But what did we expect? We learned after the shooting, as we watched the institution collectively gather, guarding against us, a possible foe, that the citadel must survive with as few casualties as possible. Have we come to expect, no demand, cures for our ailments? The *known* illnesses are treated, cured, patient released. Those who present a different puzzle, a non-responsive illness, become the files in the back room, the *cold cases* of the medical profession.

Chapter Twenty-five

Medical treatment

The professional people we encountered along our journey throughout your illness, LJ, varied from the ridiculous to the sublime. There were doctors who walked away from your struggles to recover from an OD with comments like: "I don't have time for the likes of you! I work with people who are trying to live!"

Or the comments from Dr. Carson, your last doctor: "I would have called in a witch doctor if I thought it would help." (And she called in a Shaman, but you backed out the last minute.) *If only...* laments echo. If only you had met her in the beginning.

The fractured professional medical approach to your problem, the divisiveness of the branches of psychological medical treatment: Freudian, drugs, shock treatments, bio feedback, wet packing...you experienced them all. Did any of them relieve your pain?

Was it the comfort of denial that prevented me from accepting your death as a possibility? Wouldn't even consider it! I never treated you as anything but normal, even standing by your bedside watching you struggle to *come back* my thoughts were, *"this too shall pass."* I never saw you dead. Was my denial that strong? Mentally, you survived every attempt. How many times?

Are today's families treated with the same suspicion, disregard by the medical profession as we were? Considering the *specialty* (psychology) of the medical field we dealt with, I have always questioned some of the doctors' rather calloused treatment we received. Are parents still considered the *cause?* Was it because you were of age? *Patient privilege* seemed to be their mantra, an excuse for not including us. We were rarely informed as to their diagnosis or treatment. Yet that didn't make sense since they needed our signature to commit you and agree to *pay* their bills.

From so many we received the unspoken judgment that *we* were the culprits, the virus causing the illness. Could they have been right? Would it have been better to totally disconnect from you? To leave you out there in a world that seemed so hostile to you…sink or swim?

Our hearts were always so heavy, those years we visited you in the variety of institutions. You stood out amongst the other pa-tients, so normal (or so it seemed). Life was slipping though us all, time—the sand in the hourglass of our lives.

We weren't the only ones that saw you as *normal.* Your illness was never obvious, LJ. Our friends would run into you and they'd say, "It's great to see LauraJo doing so well!" So many patients in all the different institutions thought you were *staff.* It is only in reading your journals that I realize how very much you suffered. How did you swallow your tears, put on a smile? Were we so full of denial? How could every OD be a surprise to us? Believe—we wanted so desperately to believe.

In all the time you were hospitalized, how many actual hours of treatment did you receive? It varied in each institution. In the Institute of Living, it boiled down to one and a half hours a week with the doctor. *Treatment* consisted of locking you up, side rooms, constant watch, crafts, sometimes group talks and drugs—your biggest nightmare.

At Strong there were private times provided for you to talk with a nurse, which was often more beneficial for you than time spent with the doctor, and oh so many hours to think and write. You were on *constant* a good share of the time, a safety procedure protecting people from themselves. What else can you do for highly suicidal people? I have no answer. I discovered the following letter in your chest, written so many years ago when you were in The Institute of Living. Did my letters do more harm than good?

December 3, 1980

Dear LauraJo:

Here it is Wednesday...I'm not sure what happened to Monday and Tuesday. I think about you and try to sort through the thoughts and feelings I have. I'm sure sharing them with you has its plusses and minuses.

Only by seeing how nervous you were with us do we realize what it takes for you to make yourself see us. Please don't feel that you must. We know a lot of this is complicated by the fever of the holidays, but that is something we all must work out on our own. Ron and I must learn to share the holidays with each other for although there will be years that we will all manage to get together it is going to become more and more difficult as each of you go out and make a life of your own. We know how sensitive you are to our happiness, but, LauraJo, these past couple of years must make you realize that each of us is responsible for our own happiness and although others around us contribute, it is solely within us. The wino sitting on the doorstep downtown is not necessarily unhappy and neither is Joy with all her money and good looks necessarily happy. We appreciated you sharing with us what you had written about yourself. What you said is all true, but, LJ, read it again and ask what is missing. It is evident that you see yourself as you depict...the heroine of a tragedy. Do you want to continue in this role, or would you rather be a heroine in life's great struggle?

Anger. When you were little we were so caught up in our parental role of trying to teach you what was and what wasn't acceptable within the social framework, that it never occurred to us to ask why you were so angry? Or to tell you that it was alright to feel anger. Why didn't I ask you how you could handle the hurt of rejection so nonchalantly? I asked myself that. You appeared so much stronger than the rest of us. Is it too late? Are there a few cracks in your armor? We know you can't let all the anger come pouring out at once for that would destroy you, but if you can, keep nicking away. Put aside your concern right now for "what we will think," LJ, we are not going to stop loving you no matter what you say—communication—hat a world it would be if people could communicate with each other. The irony of the whole thing is that the pain we suffer is wrapped in our fear that people won't understand and then we continue to go on living, making sure they don't. The crucial flaw in God's creation

I talked to Dr. Kumetat and he suggested that your father and I see the social worker on a regular basis. My question was for you or me? If I thought it would help you, I'd go, but I told him that if it was for me, then I would find it more of an ordeal than a release because I didn't talk to strangers. He said that was my problem and that I should work on it. Why? I'm working on trying to communicate with you more openly, but I can see no advantage in talking to a stranger. I am not unhappy with who I am, LJ. I am unhappy with the way I have handled things with you, but basically I like me: feisty, impatient, but also loving and caring, yin and yang, good and bad.

I know you are overwhelmed by what you feel is the evil and bad in you—rite it out—dmit it and then examine it. Once let out in the light of day, I think you might discover that it isn't as evil and bad as youthink it is. I know I've said that hating your mother is such a cliché—such a cop out, yet there was a time when I hated mine and reveled in my hatred, listing all the neglected birthdays and times when she ignored my needs. Now the instances may be different, LJ, between you and me, but shake them out—he times when I was too self involved to see your needs and you were too frightened to ask. It's OK for you to resent my seeming indifference, my obtuseness. My pain is diluted by my joy, LJ—n you and your brothers, Ron, in my home, my garden, my sports. Your pain seems to be undiluted because there appears to be no joy for you. It almost seems that your joy stimulus has been blocked. It was not always so. As with most of us, you are becoming a person with good and bad traits, a person of talent, a person of intelligence who hates, loves, is jealous and generous. I have yet to meet the perfect person, but I know one thing—hey must be a colossal bore!

Christmas will be a very difficult time for you and us. We want you to do what you feel you can. Don't worry about us. Be selfish, LJ, and we will begin to build some new traditions. You will too. Incorporate and expand, change and grow. Remember the good *times from the past and build on them. There is one hell of a future for you.*

Love Ya!

Ma

Change the patterns of the past. That makes sense, but how does one disassociate herself from over twenty years of relating, of parenting? How does one change the very essence of herself to provide a new stage for a troubled loved one?

What is today's take on Borderline Personality? I discovered a book by Robert O. Friedel, M.D., *Borderline Personality Disorder Demystified (knowledge is the edge)*. It gives a thorough analysis of the disease, symptoms, treatment, myths. The book reiterates that the cause of the disorder was/is often blamed on **poor or harmful parenting:**

"Even today, although evidence points otherwise, many psychiatrists and other mental health clinicians continue to deny meaningful input from family members, especially parents and spouses, to the treatment process."

Another source from NIMH (National Institute of Mental Health) states: "*Borderline Personality Disorder* (BPD) is a serious mental illness characterized by pervasive instability in moods, interpersonal relationships, self-image, and behavior. This instability often disrupts family and work life, long-term planning, and the individual's sense of self-identity. Originally thought to be at the "borderline" of psychosis, people with BPD suffer from a disorder of emotion regulation. While less well known than schizophrenia or bipolar disorder (manic-depressive illness), BPD is more common, afflicting six percent of adults, mostly young women. There is a high rate of self-injury without suicide intent, as well as a significant rate of suicide attempts and completed suicide in severe cases. Patients often need extensive mental health services, and account to twenty percent of psychiatric hospitalizations. Yet, with help, many improve over time and are eventually able to lead productive lives."

Symptoms

"Sometimes people with BPD view themselves a fundamentally bad, or unworthy. They may feel empty and have little idea who they are. People with BPD may form immediate attachment and idealize the other person...even with family members they are highly sensitive to rejection. Suicide threats and attempts may occur along with anger at perceived abandonment and disappointments.

People with BPD exhibit other impulsive behaviors, such as excessive spending, binge eating. BPD often occurs together with other psychiatric problems, particularly bipolar disorder, depression, anxiety disorders."

Recent Research Findings

Although the cause of BPD is unknown, both environmental and genetic factors are thought to play a role in predisposing patients to BPD symptoms and traits. Studies show that many, but not all individuals with BPD report a history of abuse, neglect, or separation as young children. Forty to seventy-one percent of BPD patients report having been sexually abused, usually by a non-caregiver. Researchers believe that BPD results from a combination of individual vulnerability to environmental stress and a series of events that trigger the onset of the disorder as young adults.

NIMH-funded neuroscience research is revealing brain mechanisms underlying the impulsivity, mood instability, aggression, anger, and negative emotion seen in BPD. Studies suggest that people predisposed to impulsive aggression have impaired regulation of the neural circuits that modulate emotion.

Although it appears that the treatment for BPD today is not a great deal different from the treatment you received: behavioral therapy, pharmacological treatment, antidepressant drugs and mood stabilizers, and antipsychotic drugs; BPD has become an accepted diagnosis with more directed treatment.

Chapter Twenty-six

January 2, 1981 (Strong Memorial Hospital, Bernie Kumetat, doctor)

The New Year has come and as I reflect about the passing year I become quiet and somewhat sad. I spent all but two months of it in the hospital down in Connecticut. In all that time, I never really devoted myself to getting better. I devoted most of my time to thinking about getting out. I succeeded in that twice but it got me nowhere. I was home for June and July in which time I helped Mom landscape the lot on Brook Hollow. I knew after a week home I still needed help so I decided to go back. It was a big mistake. I was there for three more months until I finally convinced Mom and Dad to let me out. After being turned down at Sheppard-Pratt, I went home and started looking for a shrink. After five days of calling and waiting and calling some more, I decided to kill myself. I went upstairs to hang myself and the phone rang.

It was such perfect timing. It was Char. The rest is unimportant. I entered the hospital (Strong Memorial in Rochester) on Nov. 8 around 5 PM and since then I have done more work than the entire five years past.

January 3, 1981

I only hit the wall once today. My hand is still fat and purple green…

I'd be so happy if I would just quit thinking about hurting or killing myself. I really never plan on killing myself, I just think of things to do to hurt myself and if I were to die, then so be it.

January 5, 1981, 1:00 PM

Doc came back today. He came in while I was talking with Kurt. It was the three of us for a while then Kurt left and it was just Bernie and me. I talked about how I was feeling and what I was thinking. He said I shouldn't try to push suicidal thoughts out of my head. I should just let them come. He said "No" when I asked for a pass. I suppose I would have done the same thing had I been in his place.

January 6, 1981

I've been thinking a lot about giving things to people and asking myself why. I hope I'm not trying to buy their friendship or that I believe they won't like me if I don't give them things. Maybe I should stop. Perhaps it's my dislike of "things" that has me giving everything I make away. I like to be busy working on something. I need to work with my hands and create. I haven't sung my song for Karen yet. I'm putting it off until she asks me. I don't want to be depending on her to make me feel good. I want to feel good about it no matter what she thinks. I want to start liking what I do and create. To like myself more, to not depend so much on other people and their opinion of me. I care if other people like me. It makes me feel good to be cared about and loved but more importantly to love and care for myself. I've started to try and change what so many years of brain washing have accomplished. For most of my life, my peers couldn't stand me. I tried to believe they were all crazy but part of me was saying, "God, nobody likes me. I must be a jerk."

My life for the past five or six years has been different. People have started to accept me and even like me. I live with the constant fear that they'll all get to know the real me and go away so I try my damnedest to not get mad at anyone or risk them getting mad at me that they don't like me anymore and that our friendship is over, so anger really scares me a lot. I keep it inside and turn it into something else like sadness or fear but never anger and if I do let some anger out, I'm terrified I'll lose the person.

Sometimes when I get the guts to look inside and see I feel more than visualize a truth. It's like a ticking bomb just waiting to be set off. All the little annoyances, the frustrations, the disappointments, all those things which could easily turn to anger for the average person are rechanneled in me so I never have to deal with the anger, but it goes somewhere and it has to come out. Before it came out in my sports, my obsession with physical activity but now I've changed. I found I need people and I realized that my fierceness in competition drove people away. You could see my anger in my face, the way I moved, the way I put my whole being into my games.

So I began to cool it a bit and things began to change. So it really is true that anger drives people away. My life is living proof. My anger now comes out in violence to myself and even that drives people away. No matter how it comes out it seems always to have a negative effect. It's true that fighting doesn't really bring people closer together but neither does holding it inside. Perhaps it comes down to this: That anger is a very powerful emotion but if the strength of the bond is true and love real, then the expression of anger will not tear it down, so to have faith in our relationships and in our loved ones is to be free of the fear of driving them away with our anger.

January 9, 1981, 12:30 PM

Some direct steps have been taken to help me make the separation from Mom. Karen saw my gift giving as a way of expressing my feelings that I had with Ma and she is right when she points out that it is and was my way of pleasing my mother. I did always give Mom things like flowers and candy and notes and extra chores like cleaning and just being the "good daughter."

.........There are so many reasons, now that I think about it, that I gave her so many gifts. It was a way I could attempt to show her how very much I loved her where I didn't feel words would be enough. I don't really know if that was the only reason. Possibly deep down inside I felt I had to reaffirm or secure her love for me. It wasn't buying her friendship...it wasn't... Oh God I hope it wasn't. I'd never want that. So now after 23 yrs. we're trying an experiment. I'm supposed to go one week without giving anything to anybody to see, I guess, if they still like me. I'm also supposed to try to do something for myself each day...

I really keep blowing it. Yesterday I gave away an orange and today a bag of popcorn to Rose. I didn't even think about it. It's such an old habit. And talk about hard! It's a constant struggle and I'm miserable... Maybe that's because I'm not caring about myself enough...

Your creations were your expressions of love. You had such joy in creating them and they (the medical professionals) robbed you of even that. Every note you sang, poem you wrote, picture and sculpture you created came from your soul, and they contaminated you with the thought that you were "buying" love or friendship. I was incensed. How obscene to take away what little pleasure you had in life.

I take the following thoughts about art from Ansell Adams, the famous photographer, in a letter to his friend, Cedric Wright in June of 1937:

"Art is both love and friendship and understanding; the desire to give. It is not charity, which is the giving of things, it is more than kindness which is the giving of self. It is both the taking and giving of beauty, the turning out to the light the inner folds of the awareness of the spirit. It is the recreation on another plane of the realities of the world; the tragic and wonderful realities of earth and men, and of all the inter-relations of these."

January 10, 1981, 1:45 PM

I think I just hit on why I've been so miserable since my restriction started. Giving things to other people was really the only thing I did for myself. That's the only way I brought any joy into my own life. It's as if I was feeding off their pleasure. Thru them I could, for a time, feel good about myself. I guess that's because when I think about the things that I like about myself what's always first is the fact that I give as much of myself as I can. I put "me" into my songs, my wood carvings, my painting, everything I give.

I've been thinking about how I feel and what I think. In my head I realize that everyone still cares and hopes the best for me, but in my heart I feel like an old sign because when a sign is first put up everyone sees it and recognizes it, but after a while no one even sees it any more.

......Somehow I feel so lost, like my ability to communicate has been taken away and I'm left with no way to say, "Thank you."

As the good book says, "It is more blessed to give than receive," and I might add, for most of us a hell of a lot easier. There is a blessing in giving that warms the heart of the giver and it was hard for me to understand the wisdom in the denial of one of your few genuine pleasures.

I am not a good *receiver* as you well know, but I am learning. The break in the canal put me on the receiving end far beyond my "ledger" capabilities. I could never repay all the kindness that was shown, so I am learning to pass it on. So many of your gifts to me and friends were works of art...gifts of the heart...that left the receiver speechless, and perhaps at a loss to express their gratitude but also an edge--of what? Discomfort perhaps for not having the talent to return the favor? I search for the words to describe this subtle emotion.

The art of receiving. So many times I have left the giver without their proper reward: a genuine, heart-felt gratitude. The following incidences come to mind: Peggy, who made me a beautiful German chocolate birthday cake. It was obvious my simple thank you was not well expressed. "Do you know how long it took me to make that?" Or Kasumi's Japanese wedding doll. From Ken, her husband: "Do you realize how rare a homemade wedding doll is?"

That last year in high school when you were finally allowed to take shop...I am sure you felt let down when I accepted the walnut, hand-carved mirror with so little expressed awe of the delicate balance and beautiful design.

"The shop teacher said I could never inlay the mirror like that." I remember the disappointment on your face when I didn't ask about the carved legs on the small table you presented to me that first Christmas after the flood. You had made it from the maple burl your dad had saved from his father's old farm. Because you were working on it at school when the canal broke, it was one of the few tokens we had from our "other" life. You were almost defiant--your words sharp. "It took me days to laminate those legs. I had to slice the wood, wet it, and put it in a vise, careful not to break it." These words echo down the years alerting me to my failure as a receiver.

January 27, 1981

It's been real strong today, that part of me who wants to die. It plans, it waits, it stays silent because no one really wants to hear it, including me. It's enough that I know it's there sitting in its dark corner, unseen by the naked eye. Only I see it: Ugly, unspeakable. I try to deny it but that doesn't make it go away. It just waits for me to return like I have for years but I just play with death as though it were a toy. It can't win now because I'm stronger. I tease it but at the last minute I break away, a flash of strength and of fear. Whichever I don't know. I don't really see myself dead, just dying and fighting. I see the anger coming out, the rage. I must kill that. Kill it before people see, before I see.

My visions of dying are so vivid and clear. I see unbearable pain and suffering. I see myself changing my mind but it being too late and I am scared and sad and lonely.

I can't explain it. I know I've tried desperately to but now I'll try again. It's like something psychic. Like an image or impression from no particular place and it hits me w/no warning nor situational stimuli. It is unknown, free flying grief, a deep, deep despair that alights on me as the wind would balance a leaf on a stone. And it sits there and covers me for a time; I am in darkness and the pain is that of a mother holding her dead infant, so deep, so seemingly everlasting and my heart feels as though it is being ripped from my very being and then I take a deep breath and the wind may blow and then I can see the sun again and it's alright…I don't know how long it will stay or how dark it will be but the frequency, though varied, is continuous in its erratic nature. Like being in a crowded room and someone, unknown, has an electric cattle prod and they're after you for some reason. You know you're going to get it, just not for how long and how hard…and you can't even see their face.

Where does despair go when the screams of a tormented soul leave their lips? Where do the unshed tears fall, and the moans for lost loved ones go? They are powerful cries of the soul and the soul is an undying entity so, tell me, where do these bits of anguish fly away to? Now I wonder if somehow there is a chance that almost like a radio antenna, I pick up these cries…as if somehow since birth I've been tuned into that frequency. I know Ma always told me sometimes I just cry and cry when there seemed to be nothing wrong. She'd fed me, changed me, held me, loved me and still I'd cry.

I compare it also to someone w/narcolepsy (sp?) sleeping sickness. You're talking to them and bam, in the middle of a conversation they fall asleep so fast…do they know why?

Observation LJE: I cling to my pain with a Sense of duty…God forgive me.

It's just that it's so real and never in my life have I had reason to feel this depth of despair and yet I know what it is I'm feeling. Sad beyond words, lost w/out hope, yet it comes and goes as the wind and gosh, is it exhausting. I do think Laura has something to do w/it. She's always angry and sad, that's why I try to ignore her so much and when I'm in a good mood and say, "Well, Laura, is there anything you'd like to get together on?" Well, I end up crying. No wonder she's never invited to parties! (a little sarcasm there.)

She tugs and whimpers at my sleeve (Laura) till I can stand it no more then I either slap her across the room or bring her in close and allow her to cry, but her pain is my pain, her tears, my tears and this woman cries. Sadness turns to despair and the pain of the hurting child I hold becomes my own. We get thru it tired and relieved and I mistakenly think it is past for now but then a growing anger, frustration follow and hurting myself becomes the thought on my mind.

Author note: (**Laura** is referenced throughout the journals… the *spoiled, controlling* child within.)

This cuts deep as I had thought we'd worked it thru and had bypassed the need to hurt anyone anymore. Disappointment swelled but with the help of the nurses conversations and a couple PRNS I held it together enough to sleep for a while. I'm down but not beaten and I'm gonna keep trying in every positive way I can.

Deepak Chopra explains the inner child more clearly in his book, *Reinventing the Body, Resurrecting The Soul:* "I know that the phrase *inner child* has been romanticized as an ideal of innocence and love…but your inner child has a shadow self that embodies the tactics of an angry, wounded, selfish infant. When your ego dips into those shadow energies, they impel you to act in very regressive ways.

"It is hard, as a well-adjusted adult, to face the fact that you are harboring a shadow that's not only destructive but childish and irrational too. Yet something positive is close at hand once you make it through the shadows."

You were swallowed up by those shadows, LJ, in spite of all your courage and valiant effort to move into the light.

February 2, 1981

I had a few internal screams tonight and it frightened me. It just reminded me of the moments of desperation. It's this super intense feeling that I can only explain as an internal scream, a desperate thrust outward. It has been there before, inside me, strong. Like when I stood up in front of that cop and pointed my gun right at him and when I sat up in the hills and swallowed all those pills, or like when I sat in Granny's garage but that time was different. I didn't want to die. I got scared. I fought. It's that part of me that has gotten me through so many times, so many "close calls." I'm playing a losing game if I keep it up. I've already gotten my share of miracles

Bernie's going slow and cautious with me. It's as if he can see what's really going on inside of me. I seem to be able to convince nearly everyone else that I'm about ready to go, to get a job, to separate from Mom and Dad, to live on my own, to be independent. But beneath all the smiles and plans for independence, there lies a very deep and intense fear of failure. Not failure to get a job, or my own place or any of that but failure to say goodbye, to separate, to like myself, to want to impress me first and then others if I choose. I'm afraid of needing people and loving people and even more afraid of them loving me. It is such a terrible dilemma to be in, to want and need love and at the same time to run away from it. I suppose it happens to many, many people. I'm not alone.

Chapter Twenty-seven

And so the years slipped by. We had wonderful, normal moments in all the struggle—the changing of medications, doctors, diagnosis, institutions. You were valiant in your determination: working with L&L, at Wegmans, teaching tennis. Your questions went unanswered as you suffered.

January 19, 1983, Wednesday, 9:09 PM

Sometimes I feel that whatever seems to be ailing me is as terminal as seriously malignant cancer. But when a cancer patient dies after years of pain, struggle, chemotherapy and whatever else, they get a gold star for their valiant efforts.

Here I've been struggling for 8 years nearly, had my own pains, emotional and physical, been in intense therapy and to special hospitals but if this kills me (meaning I give in and kill myself) there will be far from "gold stars." It will be anger, hate, disappointment. I will have "failed" in everyone's eyes except perhaps Bernie and Char. Hell! I don't expect sympathy or three cheers, but I hardly deserve condemnation for my efforts. Whatever the outcome I gave my all. Isn't that worth something, world…God? Isn't it?! Please…

January 20, 1983, Thursday, 9:00 PM

Last night I lie awake with a pain in my heart as deep as the darkness of space. I cried out under my covers and wept as quietly as I could. The pain of the soul is so immeasurable, so indescribable, it's as unique as the individual, as special and different as God's every creation and so I, as everyone is, am alone.

Yet last night I could not take it all alone so I reached my hand skyward and I asked the love of Christ to touch my hand, flow down my arm and let me feel its presence. There was no miraculous wave of joy, no sudden realiza tion of life's great worth but finally after hours of struggle and thoughts of death, I slept. …..have been having a lot of dreams lately where I'm being chased. They're out to get me (whoever) and I'm running for my life. Often they're so sure they've got me and I fly away. It's fun and exciting, especially when I get away.

Today Bernie said I had everything in me to turn that lonely empty chasm inside me into something beautiful. I could fill it w/me but he also knows that I have it in me to die too.

If I ever screw up bad and need to be locked away or die I sure hope Mom and Dad talk to someone like Bernie.

Ma and Pa left Friday …Kathy not home…went home… put away the hose to CO myself w/put away the razor blades…got out the pills…

…..took 70 extra strength Tylenol about 8:30…started barfing around 1:30 AM called Life Line about 2:30 AM…called

Perinton Volunteer ambulance myself...kept barfing every 15 min. No Ipecac necessary. Put a tube down my nose twice and an IV in my arm...made me drink Mucamyst or something like that...Dr. Haight, Dr. Wiegers and Dr. Zink came in and told me "I very well might die." Suggested I give them permission to do a Hema Profusion where they stick needles, tubes actually into your (my) groin (the main artery and vein in your upper leg), take all my blood out and filter out the Tylenol then put it back. They told me I'd most likely die if I didn't let them do it...so I did. It took about 6 hours in all and was terribly uncomfortable but so is slow death by liver failure I'm told. After that I had to take that disgusting antidote for 3 days every 4 hrs. Uck! But it must have worked. Something did because once again the drs. were wrong. I didn't die. In fact, my liver is fine.

February 2, 1983, Wednesday, 10:00 PM (Moving to my new apartment)

Great day! Got packed, took me till almost 9:00. Will have about 8 loads to take up. Only one suitcase of clothes.

Am real anxious. A little scared, too. Don't know why. Ma says they'll help me out w/$200/mo. I'll not touch it unless I have to. They're going to the lake this weekend but I should be in my pad...I'm going to make it one day at a time...tomorrow I sign a twelve week lease...it's an end and a beginning...a sunset and a sunrise. A joyous sound and a mournful cry. It is life.

February 5, 1983, Saturday, 2:00 PM

I finally got a diagnosis for myself. It is: Moderate biological depression compounded by severe emotional instability!

The instability makes it impossible, almost, to cure the first part of the depression.

….I ODed again last night but I took Bernie's advice and used junk food. Candy, donuts, pop, ice cream. All of it. Yuck! But…no long term effects.

I heard today that Karen Carpenter, the singer, died. How sad. I mean I really felt sad. Maybe that's a good sign that I felt bad about it. Death that is. Who knows, maybe it's just a rumor. I don't get a paper or watch the news.

(For Karen Carpenter)

I meant to write a letter
Of admiration to you.
For giving this world your heart songs
With a voice so pure and true,
Heart songs of sorrow sung with a smile
Lovers unfaithful and blue
You sang them as though
They were old friends
Painfully sad but true.
I meant to say how special
Your music is to me
How every time I hear you sing
The tears well up in me.
Tell me how can I love someone
I never ever knew
And tell you now though you're gone
My world is less without you.
I still sing along when I hear you
And I pray for your spirit now free
As I send you love from many
But most of all from me

Chapter Twenty-eight

When you chose to return to Taylor Manor, your father and I felt vindication in our decision to turn your healthcare over to you. I believe the benefits you received from these hospitalizations were greater than our committing you against your will.

March 4, 1983, Friday, 8:43 AM

Here I sit back at Taylor Manor after a 7-hour drive yesterday morning. I came up alone in body but not spirit. So many wish the best for me, even myself for a change I think. It was hard coming back but I know in giving up my freedom for a while I will hopefully gain more in the long run....

I'm trying hard to do everything I'm supposed to even if I don't want to. I didn't bring any pills and before I checked in, I took the razor blade out of my wallet. Good girl! No games, just honest hard work! One God blessed day at a time! We can do it! Yea...

March 4, 1983, Friday, 10:45 PM (A record productive day, 2 Parnate)

I started on Parnate 2-10 mg. group therapy...heavy duty session. Read the entire book called "Love is Letting Go of Fear". Very interesting, profound, food for thought...spoke very strongly about how we choose our feelings, emotions, actions. We have a free will and we choose so we really are what we think... Guess what....I made up with Laura. She never was the problem. It was my perception of her. We're friends and I love me, her included and she loves me. I could tell by the look in her eyes. We held each other so tightly and together we took down the wall, one brick at a time till we stood close together. I got down on my knees and we were face to face. There was no hatred or anger, just love and forgiveness. My work shall continue for even though it's terribly painful I feel more whole afterwards, more loving more real...

March 5, 1983, Saturday, 6:42 PM

"I can't figure out why you're here. You're one of the happiest people I've seen."

"You drove yourself down? Anyone who can do that doesn't need to be here..." Maybe I should listen to the other patients and I'd realize I'm fine. How very much they can't see or perhaps it's better put, "How very much I can't see!"

Group therapy was uncomfortable as usual...started talking about Mom and how things were when I was little in Oregon. It hurt so bad to tell the things Mom had told me about her childhood, how awful it was. How I swore to be so good as to make it all better (swore to myself). She shared so many things w/me, things I obviously couldn't handle from where I am now anyway.

There was so much anger. They asked me why I hit myself and who did I really want to hit? "Mom." I said softly, but added that it would help me express my anger if she'd been all bad, for there were the times she and only she would come to my rescue, take my side even if she didn't realize I was wrong. I couldn't tell. If I'd lost her, I'd have had no one…

What tales did I tell you that you thought were so awful? When you asked about my mother I probably told you that I never lived with her much, that my sisters and I were often separated and farmed out, that I never knew my father, that we had to do a lot of chores…awful? The *awful* part remains buried but perhaps from your point of view what I took for granted was *awful.* It never occurred to me that telling you that Macarthur, our pet turtle, got lost in the lettuce patch, that the drainage ditch we had to jump going to school was *full of quick sand* (according to my cousin*).* Those were the funny stories in my mind, but for a child, perhaps they were scary or sad or *awful.* Strangely enough, I can't remember talking much about my childhood…to you or the boys. If you asked questions, it was our habit to answer them as honestly as we could--how old were you?

Lessons Taught and Learned

What is a parent's obligation toward their children? I believe we are each other's teachers, for I learned as much from you as I tried to teach you…mainly how to be independent. Both your father and I thought you would fly the highest with all your talent and dedication.

Mr. and Mrs. Hodges, my foster parents, were my teachers. It was with them that I began to learn that *cleanliness was next to Godliness*, that you didn't get to play until your work was done, that *Waste Not Want Not* meant turning off lights, closing doors, eating all the food on your plate whether you liked it or not, and using a minimum amount of water in the bath.

It was from Mrs. Hodges that I learned to change my under-wear every day, air out the bed before making it, and to *wash* my face and not wipe the dirt on the towel. We (other welfare girls) cleaned the house every Saturday from top to bottom, dusting over doorjambs and along the molding.

From her I learned to cook homemade noodles: no recipe, you just fill the bowl half full of flower, add a couple of sprinkles of salt, and make a well in the middle. Then you add two eggs (trying not to get any shells in the mix), and with a fork start stirring— very slowly. I watched her and grew impatient with the tedious stirring. "Let me try!" I insisted. I knew I could do it better. The next time she made noodles she called,

"Patty, do you want to make the noodles?"

I was eager to show her how efficient I could be. When I got to the *very-slowly* part I decided to speed up the process by whip-ping the eggs into the flower. Results? Disaster! Hard little sticky lumps. A mess. As I was about to throw it out, she took the fork, made another well into the lumpy flour, broke in two more eggs and started mixing *very slowly:* Patience.

I learned to garden from JM, gather the eggs without getting attacked by the chickens, and help with the milking or tried. The cow didn't like my fingernails and showed her discomfort by kick-ing me off the stool.

All these lessons I passed on to you three insisting that you do your chores before you played, that you were not wasteful, that you took care of your toys and sporting equipment. You and the boys learned to sharpen your skies with your father. He taught you how to use his tools when you showed an interest those early years when your creative talent became apparent. How old were you when you declared you were going to *make* your Christmas gifts? Eleven, twelve? I expected popsicle sticks and colored cardboard.

"There's Jeff's," you said setting before me a perfect little miniature (3 inch) skier made of balsa wood carved with an exactor knife, perfectly proportioned, weight shift caught in an angled turn. Awe? Speechless. And you proceeded to build your father on a Sailfish, wind caught in the sail that you had created from paper stiffened with glue, painted blue and white with a center dagger board that lifted up and down. I was the bonehead tennis player, you the basketball player, and Kurt the soccer player, including shoes with tooth-pick spikes. All of the figures you created were hung from a perfectly balanced mobile that still dances near our patio door catching the wind, all of us turning, caught in that perfect time of our lives.

That was the beginning of your surprise creations that never ceased to amaze me, but did you know? I had no words to express how very moved I was by your talent and so I remained silent and you never knew—never knew the disbelief I felt in the perfect recreation of the house in Pittsford that had been part of the Underground Railroad system to assist blacks escaping from the south. Your reproduction was created from photographs you had taken. Your three-by-four foot replica was mounted on a piece of plywood, exact in every detail from railings to porticos. It was for a school-wide social studies contest. How old? Were you in the seventh, eighth grade? We couldn't believe that you didn't win a prize. The teachers said it was much too complicated for you, that your father had built it! **"Unfair!"** I echoed your sentiments.

Sculptured Feelings.

SFculptured Feelings

by Laura Jo Engebrecht

specializing in the expressive/original sculpture

Another Fine Custom Product of L & L Developers 924-4444

So many hours spent creating your sculptures molding your emotions: melancholy, love, friendship—relationships. Your creations echoed the condition of your heart. Sculptures of clay and wood--a bird in flight, a mother holding a child, a sobbing figure holding the limp form of a small dog.

The same haunting questions became the words to your songs. This darkness creeping *into* or maybe it was *out from* a suffering that we could not understand or share.

"Eat, you'll feel better!" says the Jewish mother. *"Do!"* was my admonition: run, ski, play tennis, sing songs, scrub the floor, plant the garden was my solution. Like the women whose husbands were lost at sea, or sons at war—scrub the floor, keep busy, don't think! Where did I read that exercise was the anesthesia of the mind?

Chapter Twenty-nine

Observation LJE: Choice: optimism, pessimism, realism. Which shall I choose? It is a matter of choice. Just as laughing vs. crying is a matter of choice. Life is short and though full of frustrations and disappointments it is too brief to allow yourself to sink into depression. I have wasted years in self-doubt and sadness. "No more!" I cry. It is time to surrender to the happiness God meant me to have.

March 8, 1983, Tuesday, 9:30 PM (3 Parnate)

Well I've taken a few steps backward. Sunday I tried my routine. ...I stayed in my room alone and tried to work it out till it became so unbearable...I had the urge to go to staff, but didn't. Big mistake! I sat down in front of the desk, leaned over and started pounding my head on the edge. It's so tough now but it broke thru quite readily and I got what I wanted, blood all over the place. I let it drip all over my hands and on the floor and when it would stop I'd pound some more. I knew I really should stop…got up and kicked the radiator since there was no "call" button in the room. Had to kick it 4 or 5 times before anyone came and when they did I just asked to go to "time-out" for some safe space…There was blood all over my face, the desk, the floor and my hands…they put in 16 stitches.

Next talked to Dr. Hirsh, Monday…put me on "S.O." strict observation…I hurt so intensely. I cried and cried. I felt so desperately alone. I felt like a little girl again but Mom wasn't there. She had left me. Oh pain. I was never secure w/her love, my only love. Afraid always that I'd be a bad girl, that's she get mad at me and not love me anymore so I'd save my allowance to buy her presents, I'd make their bed, I'd do the dishes after her parties. I'd keep my room all clean and neat. I tried so hard. I know I didn't have to do all that for her love but I must not have felt sure of that. I did it.

Throughout your journals, over and over, you speak of your fear of losing my love. What subtle message was I sending you? Why did you have such a consuming need to be *special* not only with me but with your friends? Human love is full of paradoxes… never quite free of the Ego demands. Our love was not enough for you.

In Dr. Ekhart Tolle's book, *A New Earth*, he speaks of the Pain Body, an accumulation of old emotional personal pain, or one that came from the *tribe* or former life if you believe in such a thing…a negative emotion from experiences that are not fully faced. Did you bring your pain with you into this life, LJ? When you were young, you had a lot of personal rejections. With each additional incidence, actual or imagined, did your pain body grow until it overcame you? I pause in my remembering. So many have survived personal horrors. Why did you succumb to what seems difficult but not the disasters so many have experienced?

March 11, 1983, Friday (3 Parnate)

....started beating up on myself: arms, legs, whatever I could reach....I'll say it's from volleyball.

At 10 AM went to my intro to bio-feedback...interesting...I go back to the hospital to get my stitches out...

March 18, 1983, Friday, 7:45 AM (4 Parnate)

Wednesday night got progressively more difficult. Finally I made the choice to play "hang-myself" in the bathroom. Spent the rest of the night in time-out...I cried a lot, felt a lot, hurt a lot, and came to the conclusion that I do such serious stuff to myself so that I can go someplace (i.e., the hospital) where people will take care of me. Dad was not around much and Mom was more friend, sister and (get this) daughter, than my mother...

I ask again, just what is a mother? I am reminded of an incident with our neighbor, Betsy. We traveled together to Boston, me on business and Betsy to visit her sister. We sat in the living room and I listened to these two women talk about their mother.

"She was great, a wonderful mother. She told me my job was to study and learn and she took care of all the chores. She was a pillar of the community, volunteer of the year. Took care of Dad..." Betsy went on and on. I watched her sister in her agitation.

"Pillar of the community is right! She had more time for the bum on the street than she had for us. Where was she when I needed someone to talk to? At some committee meeting, or lunching with town dignitaries."

It was evident they were talking about the same woman. Can anyone be all things to all people?

March 21, 1983, Monday, 4:00 PM (1st day spring; 5 Parnate)

I finally blew up this morning and told them no more one on one. It has been long enough. The bitchy nurse I had quit...talked to Dr. Hirsh. He said he didn't realize it was so expensive...too risky to take me off...I retorted I wasn't going to pay for it anymore!...I told him he's just aiding me in reinforcing my negative behavior, but he sees it as a necessary evil I guess.

I'm still working hard, listening to my tapes, reading, praying, determined to get better and getting there every day.

March 31, Thursday, 7:20 AM

...another Raa Raa cheerleader letter from good ol' Mom. I got a notice from MCC about applying for financial aid.... Jean asked if I'd ever considered asking her not to write but I'd get no mail then and really feel unloved...

I started picking and biting my sores again. By now they were pretty raw. I went up to a table alone and poured salt on them. Talk about pain.

April 1, 1983, 11:40 AM

Saw Dr. Hirsh. He asked me if I was ready to change my occupation yet, from expert professional suicide attempter to something w/more of a future. Perhaps I could strive to be the best hang glider flier or female mountain climber... he said we'd just stay w/the present therapy set up and increase the Parnate from 50 to 60 mg/day. Big deal. My faith in meds has increased very little....Oh Dr. Hirsh felt my relationship w Frank was/is detrimental. Says it's the "blind leading the blind." He pointed out that between us we only have one good eye!

Last night was a therapeutic but painful night. I had fleeting self-destructive thoughts and decided to say, "Stop, and get in touch w/the real pain." It wasn't that hard. So I got in touch w/feeling very scared and lonely and I got that old 5 yr old kid's pout on my face where my lower lip used to drag to the ground and I whimpered and whined and cried. I was relieved no one had heard me. It passed and I went to sleep.

April 27, 1983, 10:37 PM

I thought up a great new game today called: Neck-tie. Equipment consists of one army belt, the kind w/the buckle that has the flap w/the teeth. The object of the game is to crunch it down as tightly as you can and see how long it takes you to get it undone. Being this type of belt, it is very difficult. You may use anything available to get it off as long as the belt is not damaged in any way such as cutting it or bending the clip. Calling for help is strictly against the rules and results in disqualification, automatic loss and humiliation. All comers are welcome and play may continue till those involved are either bored or dead. This game is a definite must for today's thrill seeker or those who just like to tread on thin ice! Good luck. May the Farce be with you.

July 31, 1983, Sunday, Taylor Manor, Maryland

Sometimes the pain seems almost unbearable but I must be stronger than I think because I bear it. I cry, I sob, I let it hurt and then it subsides for a while… My discharge date is Aug 10. I have an appoint w/a doc. Leibowitz in NYC on Aug 11. Char got me in touch w/this guy for me. He's supposed to be one of the best in the field of A-typical depressions...

I feel all these years (8 now) that I've just taken and now I really want to start to give back. I owe so many so much. I only wish they all knew how very grateful I am to them all... Char, Pat M, Karen B, Lisa D., Dr. Pleune, Dr. Scarborough, Dr. Hirsh, Dr. Kumetat, Dr. Sobel even cuz she did try, Dr. Howard and oh so many more drs and nurses who patched me up and encouraged me to go on. They may think I'm not grateful but they just don't know how much.

I used to dream that someday I'd become a famous singer and I'd do a free concert to benefit Strong Memorial Hospital and Blue Cross/Blue Shield. Oh swell, God said it's the thought that counts? I wish that were always true, but alas, I may never be able to thank them all appropriately. That breaks my heart worst of all.

Lots of people raving about how talented I am. Want copies of my songs and poems. Selling lots of sculptures too. Real ego trip--even lucrative but still empty aching pain in my heart. So where do I go from here. I'm running out of roads to try. I could try sex and drugs and drinking but I don't think that would help either...

August 2, 1983, 10:05 PM

I feel between a rock and a hard place. So far during almost my entire hospitalizations we have dealt w/my need for attention, to be treated special, to be taken care of and how I can go about getting those needs met in a non selfdestructive or self-diminishing fashion.

What we have not looked at is the fact that those are not what I feel are the major reasons. Sometimes I feel so depressed and hopeless, so alone and afraid that I need a "most dangerous game" to distract me. A form of Russian roulette. Death as a possibility for not having to face life and its accompanying frustrations and pains. Cop-out I know but seemingly necessary at times.

I never feel out of control but do realize I choose irrational solutions to my problems and anxieties. Rather drastic forms of distraction so to say.

My choices are rather unexplainable too. Self-destructive actions that would lead to a slow, terrible, painful death if death at all. And upon this pain is piled the guilt of self- demeaning stature of an emotionally troubled, selfish, Narcissistic young woman who is forced to be exposed, (thru her own actions) to the judgment of professionals and friends soon to be x-friends, pushed away by the continual self destructiveness. So what explains the need for such an awful pastime? An essentially "sick hobby," yet potentially lethal?

I've thought of it often as my penitence for some past, hideous offense. Don't ask me what. Not being perfect perhaps. Whatever, it is self-inflicted judgment and sentencing. Sometimes beating on myself brings the relief that a devout Catholic must feel after saying their required Hail Mary's.

We have not addressed this at all. As far as staff is concerned here, it is 99% for attention. Oh how wrong they are but no one can tell them that. They have their minds made up.

...soon I fly the nest. I go either back to Roch, to NYC, or to the Cape w/my folks. ...I did find out that I qualified for

SSI today. $304.30 a month to help out. Wow…one week. It's going to be hard. I'm nervous. Maybe I should go see "Flash Dance" again…that psyched me up. It's so hard at night. I feel so pessimistic, but morning usually (always so far) has come and it finds me feeling more hopeful…I need some serious sex therapy!

September 30, 1983, 11:30 PM

I wish "better" were longer lived. I feel it at times, hopeful, optimistic almost even enthusiastic (dare I use the word). I have lost count of all the times I have dreamed of overcoming this and sitting down to write one of the inspiring books of struggle, courage and strength so admired by those who've never gone thru such ordeals. Except now when I see such tales on the TV or at the movies and reviews of such books, I just want to puke. I don't want to hear, see, have it rubbed in my face…"See, I did, now why can't you!" Inferior? Don't want to get better eh? Want more attention? Want sympathy? You slime, you could do it if you really wanted to. You've done everything else you really wanted to do so that pretty much settles it. You, LauraJo, don't want to be better…well…independent… successful…at peace with yourself so you create pain internal and external

At night it is so very bad. I lie awake and it feels like a great giant is twisting his heel into my chest. My heart feels like it will burst. The tears stream down and I want to scream and then all I want is to go to sleep and never wake up. Mom and Dad and the family, they love me so much but I swear sometimes that makes it hurt even more. The guilt is almost unbearable.

I have never understood guilt, LJ. Why? I have no clue, but recently I read that *guilt* is the Mafia of the mind. That certainly was true for you,

FREEDOM

They say I won't be able to make
It work. They say I'm not ready,
But my heart cries out for freedom
Even though I know the walls are
Inside I desire to break them
Elsewhere. Stone by stone
I will tear the walls down until
I lie naked in the sun.
Born into a new tomorrow
While yesterday's memories are
Only a shadow of what was.
I will never forget the trials
But the pain will be dulled
By the passing years and
I will smile at each dawn.

Chapter Thirty

Monroe Community College Fall, 1983

We were optimistic. Things appeared to be going well. You filled out the application and went off to class. I remember that first day. You were discouraged. "I don't think I can do it, Ma. I think I'm brain damaged." I certainly couldn't argue with you about that possibility.

"Try it for a couple of weeks, you have time."

And so you went. Each day became a little easier than the last or so I thought. Reading your journals, I now know what effort it took. I discovered the following paper in your chest. Your words tell your story far better than mine.

(Author's note: Teacher's comments are in bold)

Monroe Community College

Mrs. S. Waldow Formal Education Paper
Sociology 101 LauraJo Engebrecht

My formal education, an extension of the socialization process, started over twenty years ago in the college town of
Corvallis, Oregon. It was 1962 when I was five years old.
I did not have to go through the trauma of stepping onto
a big yellow school bus because we lived close enough
to school to walk. My first day at school was made easier
because I was able to go with my older brother.

The kindergarten curriculum must have been the usual A
B C's and 1, 2, 3's. It didn't impress me enough to remember. I do remember the teacher. Her name was Mrs.
Chadwick. Mrs. Chadwick's authority came from more
than her position as a teacher. It also came from her sharp
voice and yard stick that she always carried which quite
often found a target on some unfortunate behind. It wasn't
long before we'd renamed her Mrs. Chadwicked. Hers
was an achieved status **(good point)**. There was no doubt
in our minds who was the boss.

It wasn't until first grade that I acquired my deviant label,
not a positive aspect in this case. I don't recall repeated
incidents of hitting my peers, but I do recall the bribe my
mother put forth to entice me to stop it. I'm sure spank
ings were tried first, but they didn't work. I must assume
I stopped my aggressive, deviant, antisocial behavior as
I received the "surprise" as my parents called the "give-
ashow" projector they had promised me if I would conform.

I remember interacting sociably at school during recess
and walking to and from school. Mostly I stayed with my

brothers when they'd let me or Mom when they didn't want me around. I did not like school. It was just a place I was supposed to go, a place to go to wear the clothes I'd laid out the night before--a place to try to get along. I preferred to take my "give-a-show" projector into the closet and watch cartoons on the wall until I burned out the batteries.

I've thought a good deal about that incident. I cannot remember hitting people. A few weeks ago I asked my mother if it was near the time they were planning the move to New York from Oregon, a strange place that I could not even pronounce. I asked if she had told me at this time. She couldn't remember even talking to us about the move. I do remember I was rather scared and sad about it, but I had no choice. We left Oregon in January, 1965.

I was seven and one-half years old and cold. I wondered if we had moved to the Arctic. I remember that first day I walked into Mrs. Pillsberry's second grade class—all those faces staring at me while she introduced the "new girl." This little girl came up to me and asked if she could be my best friend. I didn't know what to say, but I think I said "sure."

Those early years of my formal education set the pattern of a struggle that would continue for the most part of my education. I was having a very difficult time making the change from significant other, namely mother, to the generalized other, my peers. The closest I could get to them seemed to be as a friendly acquaintance. Only my mother was my friend, my only true friend. I became extremely competitive with my peers. I didn't feel they like me because I wasn't invited to "the" parties. At first I competed thinking that if I won, they'd like me, respect me **(why?**

Explore this), want to be around me. My aggressive, competitive actions only put them off more. When field day (the day each class had its picnic) rolled around, that was my day. I won them all. As many events as I could enter chalking up 1st, 2nd in all of them. Un acceptance was the motivation that drove me. I ran, jumped and threw with a vengeance and drive, but if anything my success made me even less popular. As it turned out the function our class field day was supposed to fill, being fun, camaraderie and healthy peer interaction was not found here for me. It was actually more dysfunctional in that I felt more distant and alienated than ever. I still felt pride in all of my ribbons.

As time passed, I found myself at extremes with the teachers. I either adored them and bent over backward to please, both academically and otherwise; or I detested them, labeling them "power hungry, ignorant jerks" and I'd go out of my way to be a pain. It was in fifth grade that I nearly flunked a subject. That was quite new to me as I usually had no trouble keeping my grades up. I didn't like the teacher and I knew she didn't like me. It was obvious to me that she was nearly flunking me because she didn't like me. It was that year that I did my first survey research. I was counting on my fellow peers to substantiate my feelings by signing a letter to the effect that they agreed that Mrs. Wall (the teacher) "picked" on me. News of this research reached the principal and here I was, a deviant again—still, more like it. The substitute teacher that week must have found out about my survey because another girl and I were laughing in class one day and because I laughed louder (as she said) I got locked in the closet, wherein I proceeded to goof around and was told shortly thereafter, in front of the entire class that "I couldn't even act like a lady in the closet." I don't remember how many signatures I acquired on my petition. Fifth grade turned out to be a strong year for reinforcing approval of success and disapproval of failure. The teacher put up this chart for the multiplication tables 1-12 and for each one that we could stand up in front of her and successfully recite, we'd get a gold star. It was hung up in front of the room so everyone would know how everyone else was doing. Very effective. **(Why? Elaborate)**

The sixth grade was rather uneventful as I recall. I do think it was the last year I was physically aggressive for the sake of being a bully. From that time on my physical acts were in retaliation to a threat (in my own mind). My peer relationships continued to worsen. I spent recess time by myself in a restricted area outside, or sometimes I'd walk to the fence at the edge of the schoolyard and lay down in the grass. It was tall there because they didn't mow it and I could hide there and watch all the other kids play and talk. They couldn't see me. When it was time to go in, I'd wait until almost everyone was gone then jump up and run to the door before the teacher closed and locked it. I was told again and again to stay where they could see me, but I didn't care so I just finished off 6th grade and went to a new school—junior high.

What a role change this was. From being "king-of-the-hill", oldest ones in school to being the "runts" of the litter. Ninth graders thought they were soooo tough. Maybe I went against some norms regarding my peer and teacher interactions but a lot of my peers broke mores. They'd smoke in the bathrooms, cut classes all day, but they received sanctions too like suspensions, or having to stay after school for a week.

Up until this point, I'd been going along thinking I was fairly intelligent. Grades had been O.K. Teachers' comments had been fine, but here I was going into seventh grade and "regular" math while a group of kids who I felt were no smarter **(sponsor mobility)** than I were going into advanced placement math. I complained a little, but went where they told me. One thing I knew I wouldn't have to take would be Home Economics. I already knew how to cook and I didn't want to learn to sew. I didn't need any role model lessons. I wanted to take Industrial Arts. It was 1969. Weren't women liberated yet? I pleaded, I begged. I even baked cakes for the principal. No luck. The law said I had to take Home Ec. I hated it. What did I learn? The lettuce I like best was called "Iceberg"!

I think at this point my aggressive Id was feeling that it sure would be nice to be popular so my ego thought about it for a while and came up with a plan and my super ego went ahead and joined as many clubs as possible **(?)**

In the seventh grade I was an officer in student government, a member of band, intramurals, Yorker Club (history club) school newspaper, drama club and Camp Fire Girls. I started to meet new people, even made a couple friends. I don't even want to go into the catastrophes of that year, but it didn't work. I still wasn't popular (I have a feeling my expectations were a bit high.) I wasn't even accepted. I think my non acceptance was due to the fact that my self image and personality were significantly different from the way my peers experienced me. **(Important!)**

I don't recall much about the eighth grade except my activities' list dwindled radically. So did my "couple" of friends. The one I can remember became more interested in chasing boys. I was very disappointed. I had a very socially **(explore this)** unacceptable knock-down-drag-out on the school bus one day. It wasn't my fault. I was merely defending my little brother who was being attacked. Considering I had a very small nuclear **(good pt.)** family, I was seeing a great percentage of our entire clan being assaulted. My little brother did not see the situation quite as drastic as to need my intervention. My protection proved to be more of an embarrassment to him. I regretted my impetuous action later since my peers would not let me forget it.

In the eighth grade I retained my deviant label. At this point I refused to go downstairs to the cafeteria for lunch due to the continual aggravation of trying to find a place to sit. A table with eight chairs and one person was unavailable since all seats were "saved". This would happen two, three and sometimes four times until I'd end up sitting alone. It was easier and less stressful not to go down. I'd wait until the halls cleared, then I'd crawl out the window, a definite no-no. There I'd eat, read a book for just enjoy the fresh air. Come late fall and winter I started going down to the auditorium. It was dark usually, but there'd be one or two spot lights on down front so I'd sit down there and read, until one day

I got caught. The guidance counselor walked in on me. She thought I must have some real deep seeded emotional troubles (psyc vrs. soc perspective?) to prefer eating alone. She set up an appointment to have lunch with me. I tried to explain, but ended up spending forty-five minutes saying, "No, it's not like that." I was relieved when our meeting was over.

Ninth grade was big-time in junior high. I had a German teacher who infuriated me. She expected a lot and I usually gave it except for one time. I remember. I completed an assignment in a rather sloppy manner and turned it in expecting a grade no lower than a B. It came back with a "C" on it. I looked at a few of my peer's projects and got really annoyed. They had higher grades with no better work. I asked "why?" and hoped she'd change my grade. She looked at me and said, "LauraJo, you and I both know that you're capable of much more than that. You didn't work very hard to do this and I'd be insulting you if I said you had." I said nothing. I was flattered. It was true, I hadn't worked very hard. The "C" stuck, but the incident certainly improved the level of my self expectations. I was "better than average" and "capable of more." I still disliked German, but I liked and respected Frau Markham.

The biggest thrill of my freshman year had to be when I made the girls' varsity basketball team up at the high school. I played bench warmer most of that season, but I was the only freshman on a twelve-girl team. It was an achieved status. I was proud of being told I was good enough and was determined to improve.

High school seemed better. Even as a tenth grader I played first clarinet in the band and was first string starting guard on the basketball team. My values were changing a little. I'd given up the hope of ever being popular. I started dressing like the rest of my peers in sneakers and jeans instead of dresses and skirts. I would not give in on my hair. When other girls were ironing their long tresses, I insisted on my short natural hair style. I was not a trendy person. **(why?)** I went for comfort. I think, but this point, my fellow school bus riders had ceased to mock me, tease me about "what sex I wasI" and even ceased shooting spit balls at the back of my head. It was a nice change. After three years I was finally informed that I had the option to take Industrial Arts. **(how did this come about?)** I had no time on my schedule.

The spring of my sophomore year I tried out for the men's varsity tennis team. I'd played since I was twelve, competed since I was fourteen and knew I could beat all but two of the other guys trying out (my two brothers). The coach turned out to be a chauvinist pig and said I should kiss his ass (implied) for letting me be on J.V (junior varsity). This team was made up of kids (boys) who didn't even know how to score. I went home in tears and my mom was so mad she went to the head of the athletic depart ment--rather she drove me and I had the confrontation. He and the tennis coach were of the same mold. We got nowhere fast. I didn't play that year and found no moral support from my peers, teaching staff and those no good brothers of mine. As far as academics were concerned, I kept telling myself I was a good math student and pulled a 98 in geometry. It was downhill from there on with my grades. My consuming interest in high school was to be in sports both in and out of school. While the girls were looking at the guys and the guys at the girls, I was in the gym dribbling and shooting. I played an aggressive game and never let up. I was in great shape physically, but the fact that I fouled out every game by half time proved I was a bit angry about something.

The tennis coach changed and my junior year I played #3 singles under my older brother at #1, younger brother at #2. What a year! I was still starting as guard at basketball, our team won the section V championship and I made the all-star team. I even got accepted into a clic that year but I wouldn't participate when invited. I always felt out of place and afraid I'd be rejected so I just played ball and kept winning, but I still hurt inside. People still made comments about my sexuality.**(say more)** When I came to school dances, I never had a date, but I loved to dance so I'd go and I'd ask the guys to dance. I wasn't feeling any role conflict. I just wanted to dance. Sure, some of them said, "No". One guy even said "Are you kidding, with a dog like you?" I just asked someone else and my brother would always ask me.

Was rejection devastating? Obviously it wasn't as bad for me as it was for the girls crying in the rest room because no one had asked them to dance. **(Really?)** Perhaps it was just social control but because they were girls they felt like they couldn't ask a guy to dance or maybe it was their own self image at stake.

My senior year started out with a bang. Jeff, my older brother had gone off to Oregon to school and our small nuclear family was one smaller. I had managed to get the schedule I wanted by going around and asking the individual teachers if I could take their class instead of the ones the computer had given me. I'd been doing that for three years and not thinking anything about it. To me it was no big deal. I'd gotten into Industrial Arts, art class, creative writing, all those enjoyable classes I had never had time for.

It was a beautiful day when I drove home from school, a little early to beat the school busses. A sunny, warm October 29th. I came into the house and kicked off my shoes and started sorting through the mail. I was expecting letters from colleges about my applications for a tennis scholarship. My mother, who is a writer, was proofreading the re-write of her new manuscript before mailing it. Then it started, a rumbling noise, a pounding on our front door, a mad dash up the hill and in less than a minute our home was a hole in the ground. Dead fish lay all around as the waters from a break in the Barge Canal started to recede. It was as if a bomb had hit. Everything was gone. I didn't even have shoes on. Now I know how it feels to live in a war-torn country. I went to school the next day. I sat alone in the library and though of all the memories and years of work gone in an instant. I started crying then I ran out of the school and threw my books on the steps. I didn't give a damn about my school work. I started walking the five miles home.

When I got to where the expressway crosses the canal, a policeman got out of a patrol car and asked me, "Are you an Engebrecht?" I said yes and he gave me an old yearbook that had washed through the flood. It had an article about our team winning the sectionals and a piece of basketball victory net. I could barely see the photos for the mud but it was something. Shortly after that I got into a power struggle with the coach and got thrown off the basketball team. They didn't win another game and the rest of the girls were very angry at me. I let the academics slide, but still held onto my "B" average. I began going to the wood shop every morning at 8:30 and staying until 3 pm or later. I was competing in another way now, building and designing my own furniture to enter into the county Industrial Arts show in the spring. My teacher said I'd never get it done, **(why?)** but I knew I would. I stayed up all night before the show and it was done. I won two tro phies in the contest. Of course, I wasn't satisfied, because I didn't take "Best of Show."

The same clic was still trying to include me and I was still avoiding them. What I didn't realize at the time was that I was changing, becoming less obnoxious and people were beginning to like me more. They showed this at the awards assembly. The flood had washed away nearly fifty trophies (tennis) I'd won and the Class of '75 had ok'd the purchase of a plaque that had listed over a dozen of the most im portant trophies I had won. They also voted me "most athletic" which was more of an achieved status versus a gift. I was very surprised. It ended my high school education with a little sparkle of approval. I thought it might help and who knows, perhaps it did.

No scholarship arrived in the mail, so college was postponed for a semester while I helped with the building of the new house. In January of '76 I stepped onto the airplane and waved goodbye through tears and took off for Tucson, Arizona and the University of Arizona. It was hard because my mother was still my significant other, my friend, my sister and my world, but now she was beginning to push away. I might as well go to college.

Before I continue into my college education, I would like
to look back and see what types of mobility I experienced
in the first thirteen years of my schooling. I had a lot of
sponsored mobility. First were my parents. Where they
could afford to live was where I went to school. We weren't
rich, but we weren't poor either. My father was getting his
PHD and teaching, my mom stayed home and took care
of my brothers and me. We didn't have to go to a day-care
center. When we moved here, they checked out school
districts and found that Pittsford was rated quite high so
we moved into an affordable area in the district called
Bushnells Basin.

I experienced contest mobility throughout junior high
and high school. Achievement tests, SAT's, final ex-
ams, they all made up a part in deciding where I'd go
and wouldn't go. Regular math versus advanced math
for example. Other contests were in music. These
were coupled with some sponsored mobility. The band
director would select a few students **(good point)**
whom he thought would have a chance of qualifying
to play in the "all county" or "all state" band. He liked
me. I took private lessons from him—more parental
sponsoring. He picked me as one to go. Next, I had
to select a piece of music and practice to perfection.
Ha! Then go and wait in this hall with all the other
kids to audition. They were so much better. I wouldn't
have a chance. My turn. I played. Not bad. I made it!
Last section, next-to last chair. Oh well I made it anyway. This automatically gave me a chance to try for
All State, thus I'd had an experience with tournament
mobility too. If I screwed up at State, it was all over.

I had a try at some further contest mobility for a ranking on the men's tennis team. Everybody had to play everybody else. The person who was best that day was #1 and so on down the line. Throughout the year each player could challenge up a certain number of positions. If he/she won, they moved up. If they lost, they'd stay where they were unless they lost to someone below them and then they'd move down.

I could have gone to the college of my choice without a scholarship, but I wanted to help as much as I could with the expenses so I chose a western school with a tennis team. I hoped I could play high enough on it to get a scholarship. The University of Arizona seemed right. I had to play to win in try outs. The coach thought I was good enough even though I broke my ankle before I finished tryouts. She offered me a scholarship and I gladly accepted. Having that scholarship made me work a lot harder. I didn't want the coach to be sorry, so I worked hard and moved up to #1 singles.

There I was, a physical education major in a school of thirty-three thousand where I didn't know a soul. What an adventure. My classes were fine. Not as easy as most people think for a physical education major. There are a lot of required science classes. Subjects like kinesiology, anatomy, physiology. My worries were elsewhere. Finding a homier place than the dorms to reside in. Sorority rush was on. I decided to try for a sorority. Every day after tennis practice I'd arrive at the Rush parties in my sweaty warm-ups while everyone else was in their formal evening attire. I was pleased and surprised that I was invited to join two.

I chose one and found it much more like a family than the dorms. One weekend for excitement I went parachuting and broke my ankle. There went my chance for a scholarship I thought so I went to work on the books, joined ROTC and avoided all the frat parties.

I kept to myself a lot though my sorority sisters were more than friendly. It felt so good being included. I ended up with a 3.5 and a scholarship for tennis for the next year. Meanwhile that semester, the president of the sorority, a junior pharmacology major asked me if I'd like to be her roommate the following fall. It was a privilege and I was excited for I liked her a lot. My answer was *yes*, of course.

The summer passed fast with a visit from my future roommate. My older brother like her a lot and offered to drive me back to school in August. We strapped my motorcycle on the back of the car and took off. School was the same. None of my professors were very memorable. I was determined to show the coach I'd earned that scholarship she'd given me so I proceeded to work myself up to #I singles at my academic expense. I dropped to a 2.9 that semester after dropping out before Thanksgiving and then re-enrolling after break. A short-lived drop out, I didn't miss a day of class. My struggle at this point was not knowing what I wanted to do.

We had a big tournament, a dozen schools flying west to compete. I represented the University of Arizona at #1 singles. I took off on my motorcycle and stayed in the mountains above the campus. My major obligation at school was my tennis. I was getting paid and I didn't even show up. What the hell was wrong? At Christmas break I went home and played every day with better players. My academics were O.K. It was my tennis that was in trouble. I got worse and worse. If it hadn't been for my doubles play, I'd have dropped off the traveling team. I held in at #1 doubles so I could still feel like I was earning my scholarship.

My roommate and I had been getting very close. She'd run up and hug and kiss me all the time. Memories of earlier times, accusations of sexuality traits, her actions bothered and embarrassed me. **(good connection)** When I told her to cut it out, it hurt her feelings and things were never the same. I kept up the required courses, some out of sequence, but pulled a 3.2 before I left for summer break.

The next fall I still wasn't sure if I wanted to be in college, scholarship or not. I decided to ride my new motorcycle out to Arizona from New York and try to finish what I'd started. When I pulled up in front of the sorority house, I was surprised to see a slightly familiar looking girl run up and give me a hug. "You made it! You must be crazy, but you made it. We were all so worried." She became my new friend.

That semester was short. I started out by fooling the computer and taking twenty-eight credit hours. Mom had said if I just stayed busy, I wouldn't have time to get into trouble. The guidance department didn't catch up with me until I was ready to drop out again. Trying to fool the computer was some primary deviation. I'll admit but no one got hurt. I think it was sometime in October of '77 that I packed up a knap sack and took off without a good-bye to anyone. Awfully rude I know. I didn't even bother to drop my classes—twenty-eight credit of hours of "F" didn't bother me. I didn't think I'd ever go back to school. It was thanks to my friend, Carrie, that I don't have all those failures on my record.

It was about a year and a half before I returned to school. During that time I had jobs varying in pay from minimum wage for cutting cheese at Wegmans to approximately $20 an hour for organizing and running my own tennis clinics. I made enough money teaching tennis to purchase a used sports car. It was fun, but teaching tennis and cutting cheese seemed like it wasn't going to get me what I wanted out of a career. What career that was, I still didn't know, but I felt the need to go back to school. This time I chose Cortland and decided to go for sports medicine and be an athletic trainer. I hoped I was ready to settle down and get to work. I tried to keep busy, I joined the track team and was the slowest one on it, but then I was probably the oldest too.

It was January 1979. I was 21 and still recovering from a very serious self-destructive gesture (I don't like the word suicide) Hell, I didn't want to die, I just wanted to stop the pain. I thought maybe if I could get into a career I liked it would help but I was still an excitement junkie, still a deviant. One of my thrills was to ledge walk on the ninth floor. I usually went at night when no one would see me and get all upset. Well, I got caught and they said if I'd go see a counselor they wouldn't throw me out of school. I went a couple of times, but she just thought I had some sort of functional disorder. I guess I did too. I figured I was just an attention seeking, anti-social, deviant. So did everyone else. When I did it again, I was asked to leave. It was best that way because with my "nothing-matters" attitude, I had started skipping classes and was behind.

My parents picked me up from school and committed me to the psychiatric department in the hospital. I rebelled and decided to take the big leap some secondary deviation and try some real criminal behavior. Behavior that resulted in my eye getting shot in the face with shot gun pellets and losing my right eye. It was a very egoistic suicide attempt. I felt bad about involving anyone else and wrote a letter of apology to the policeman who shot me. When the police found out the circumstances, they dropped all criminal charges. My medical history plus the fact I was armed with a toy gun were determining factors in their decision.

After living the next two and one-half years in psychiatric hospitals, I tried striking out on my own and rented a room down in the city. My shrink of three years had run out of things to say to me. He believed my emotional problems were a functional disorder too and informed me that I may always feel depressed. I didn't want to hear that so I said good-bye and returned to the nurse who had worked with me back in October '78. She works closely with several doctors but also runs her own counseling business. Char was certain it was an organic disorder and treatable with meds. I was anxious to start because I'd enrolled in school for the fall of '83 at MCC. It had been a long time and I'd need all my wits to learn to study again. Career wise I was still along the same line with my sites aimed at physical therapy at Upstate Medical in the fall of '85.

I was skeptical about medicine being a major part of the answer. I'd been labeled a deviant and I had come to be lieve it, but I still wanted to try, so I started my meds in November and took them as prescribed (past attempts with medication led to overdoses.) Char trusted me and I promised her I'd not abuse them. School was work, as I expected and was hanging on by the skin of my teeth. I started dropping out of things, the group I was singing in and my volunteer job. Then I lost my part-time job for calling in sick two days in a row, but I refused to quit school. I needed to finish, even with a "D". I needed to finish.

Sometimes I'd do the work only an hour before class. I skipped one of my classes a couple of times but I hung on. Then one morning I woke up and it didn't feel like there was a ton of bricks piled on me. I felt pretty o.k. Each day that "o.k." feeling lasted longer and sometimes was a "good" feeling. My school work seemed easier, less burdensome. I even wanted to go to class. I could think about my goals more and dream about what it would be like to have a diploma to hang on my wall, but more then that, the sense of satisfaction and accomplishment it would bring along with the greater job opportunities. To me finishing school means being ready to get a job that I can support myself with. Supporting oneself is being grown up. I need to finish school so I can finally grow up.

There is no single reason for how and why I'm taking classes at MCC today. It is obvious from these pages it is a multiple causation. I thank God I still have a brain in my head to be able to go to school. The answers I seek may not lie inside a lecture hall or in some lab. More than likely, they lie within me. **(and understanding your life experiences)** Perhaps school and completing my education will be one of the tools I can use to better understand myself and my goals.

(You obviously put a lot of time and thought into this paper. Your connections to concepts we covered is strong. Nice job and keep up the good work both in side and out)

Chapter Thirty-one

October 5, 1983, Wednesday, 5:00 PM

I've got everyone fooled. I only let them see the acceptable side of me, the fun, enjoyable side that's nice to be around. That's the way I want to be w/them. I've got it figured out finally, why the last 9 years have been such hell. I'm not supposed to be here. Nine years ago at 2:15 on Oct. 29th I was supposed to die. That's why I've been so miserable for so long. I'm not supposed to be here...

Now I know that's silly. Of course I'm supposed to be here. I mean I'm here. Right? And what IS is supposed to be, Right? The car wouldn't start. The seat belt was stuck but I started it. I used my head. I stood up and it started and I escaped death (The break in the canal 1974 when house was destroyed). Maybe that was my first brush with it too. Maybe that's what started all the damn Russian Roulette games. I must have gotten something out of it.

October 13,1983, Thursday, 5:30 PM

Sometimes I wish people realized that no one in this world "wants" to die. When someone dies by their own hand, what society calls "suicide," so many assumptions and accusations fly. I'm not claiming to know the truth of each individual's reasons but I, for one, don't believe they want to die. It's just that living has become so awfully unbearable. If not externally than internally. The fear becomes overwhelming, the loneliness and hopelessness become endless and immeasurable. There seems no other alternative. They (society) like to call it a cry for help, especially when a woman attempts and fails to die. She is only looking for "attention." Perhaps the truth is more that she has a stronger awareness of not really wanting to die but wanting some help. Men aren't supposed to need help so I guess their despair may run deeper. Maybe that's why they succeed more often. Their lack of alternatives is more absolute. I am not an observer in this phenomenon. I am right in the middle. An active participant. Why? ...I suppose too that I am dealing more w/egoistic and anomic suicides, not altruistic. Those reasons go beyond my present understanding.

Sometimes I just feel like life is a bad dream that I'd like to wake up (die) from. It has its lulls of agony but it rarely gets pleasurable. That's not Gods fault, He tries to make it nice. We all just fuss and fume and make it hard for ourselves. It's almost like I don't want to feel good sometimes but I don't want to die either and I don't want to continue like this, just barely hanging on. It's not good enough especially w/as much potential as I have. My guilt is so very paramount over my other feelings. I've prayed for forgiveness but I can't feel it...even if I don't kill myself my guilt is there over my evil thoughts... "Evil" spelled backward is "Live." Maybe that's what life is all about. Maybe that's why I want out sometimes. Lord only knows.

I think she wants them to love me up. She's still playing those sex game w/the devil at night too. We dream a lot and I remember. My whole life I've had maybe 4 or 5 sexual dreams and only one of those was w/a man and it was the only one I found distasteful. The others were pleasurable only physically but the guilt was awful. I never really saw the other person as a woman but somehow I just knew it was another female. What the hell am I gonna do?

My sexuality has to come out and it wants to come out homosexually. I don't know how to change. I try to desire men but they turn me off. I don't want my space invaded so to say, but the guilt is too strong. I can't go against God. Only in the games at night and they are only games.

She wants to beat me but I say no. It won't help. She's sewing apple seeds (they have syinide (sp?) but I won't eat them. We were going to get a bag of apples today just for the seeds but I dumped them out after she picked them. Ha. She'll not win. I'm stronger. Life is stronger but she's persistent.

We think about it all the time. I don't know why she wants to hurt me bad. We went looking for good places to die to-day. I'd like it by the lake. She doesn't care. I tell her to shut up but it's no good. We feel worse before my period. She wants to quit all the time. I say "no" and do my obligations: work, school and such. I eat and sleep. I get by. I take care of me, my teeth, especially that expensive crown because I'll be around cuz she won't win and I want good teeth.

December 31, 1983, Saturday, 11:30 PM

New Year's Eve, alone again but as usual, by choice. Looking back at this year, I see the expected combination of positives and negatives. The first two months of '83 were spent in and out of Strong w/Tylenol ODs and rat poison parties. March thru Aug. 10 were spent at Taylor Manor where I worked on a variety of positive alternatives to self-destructive behavior. They included bio-feedback exercises, creative expression thru sculpture, music, talking, exercise and basic behavior modification thru a reward-punishment system. In August I met w/a specialist in NYC, Dr. Michael Liebowitz. He felt meds could be helpful but also thot I'd been treated too easily and should be sent to State for any further self-destructive actions. I met with Bernie one more time but after he said surviving and feeling crumby may be the best I'll ever achieve, I decided to look for someone more optimistic to work w/me. I chose Char and she agreed to be my therapist. I tried to make it without meds...I got into beating myself and stealing. I beat my head so bad my good eye swelled shut and I was blind for a day or two. Finally asked Char for some meds... partly to feel better, partly I wanted some meds that could easily be fatal. I stuck with school and finished the semester with an A in Sociology and a B+ in math...

My resolution? I will face life one day as it comes and I will live each day as it passes and someday, when the time is His I will die. Not before. I have so much and I know it. I do not take it for granted. I appreciate it. I do not flaunt it or revile it. I am grateful and though many will disagree I know my heart and my Father does too. He will see in secret and reward me (I pray) with forgiveness and mercy. No more than this is what I ask. Not necessarily to go to heaven but to, at least, not burn in Hell. I may have little faith at times but Lord knows I've tried. I hope that counts for something.

This past year saw more hospitalizations, a stay at the State hospital, work with your jobs, more ODs, school at MCC. We were able to talk about death openly.

January 3,1984

Jeff's starving to death in Pennsylvania. Has lost 18-20 lbs and is gaunt and awful looking just cuz his wife told him he ate more than his share of food…Damn it! If I could grab both of them and shake them till they straightened up. I'd do it but I know they have to work it out themselves. A lot of people would like to rattle my brains a little too. Hopeless case that I am! I finally believe that Dr. Sobel was right when she said I'm incapable of loving. I'm going on 27 and have never had a lover. Good friends yes but a lover, no. That would terrify me. The closeness. I…sit on my sexuality…won't let it out…can't live without it…don't want to live with it. I'm not a whole person… I'm more alone than any person… Is this my choice? Not consciously… Regardless, I am what she said, incapable of loving…

I find this very difficult to believe. Your love wrapped all of us in so many ways—through your songs, poems, sculptured feelings, love of God. You just couldn't seem to feel our love. The walls—you had built such a fortress.

January 16,1984, Monday

Here I sit watching the American Music Awards live from California. In a way, they are almost sad though this is subtly hidden beneath the wide range of extreme talent and entertainment. Mr. Michael Jackson, who couldn't be more than 25 or 26, has taken at least half a dozen awards. He is nearly speechless but behind his dark glasses and sparkly jacket, I sense a pair of sad eyes and a troubled heart. I pray for the strength he will need to bear the honor of his vast achievements. It not only takes strength to lose it all and go on, but to win it all and go on requires strength also. God give you strength, Michael, and fill up your deep need where success is not enough.

Jan. 24,1984 (letter from brother, Kurt)

Dear LJ:

Hi! How goes life in Roch? I'm back in the swing of things here in Garmisch! Ski weeks training, cross country, all the same old jazz. My legs are really sore—three weeks of just sitting around did a number on my condition. Well after this week, one more and I should be back to ground zero.

It was great to see you. It was great to spend the holidays at home. I'm sure you have tough days but as far as I'm concerned I think you've made some big strides forward towards independence and a life you can live with. I've come to the conclusion that life even for the blessed is anything but easy. We were very lucky children in that our childhood seemed blessed. Our parents never divorced. We didn't have drug problems or power struggles or anything that most kids go through. Possibly that has been our undoing. Adversity, it is said, makes us stronger and perhaps now with all the adversity in your young adulthood you've had to go through what most children learn at a younger age. Life is not always fair, there is more pain and suffering than seems bearable for some of us. Catastrophe, death and misfortune strike the most unlikely in a most unpredictable manner. But somehow man has been endowed with one emotion that allows us to keep trying—HOPE. Without it we can't survive because life is filled with disappointments if not tragedies.

Don't feel alone in your pain. The whole human race shares this most undesirable aspect of our lives. I guess the only advice I can offer is (although) compassion for others' suffering is a most noble characteristic of a man or woman, but grieving and allowing their pain to enter into our own hearts offers no solution, just more misery. If we cannot, will not, or just are not capable of helping the afflicted, then we must move on and live our own lives as in turn they also shall do and, if by chance, it is death that harms others, their struggles are now over and no amount of grief or remorse can help the situation.

Hopefully this hasn't sounded like disoriented rambling. Life really is beautiful. I love you, Laura. Don't always look for the final answers. I think we both have a tendency to do that.

All my love, your little brother,

Kurt

April 12, 1984

Told Ma today if she died before me I'd really miss her a lot…she said she'd miss me too…I think it's real unfair for a kid to die before their parent. It must be awfully hard on the parent. It's just not meant to be that way, but I'll be so sad if they go 1st. It's nice to be able to be open about it and talk freely expressing feeling of love and affection. It's tougher for Dad I think.

Death. Interesting. Intellectually we all know that death hovers over all of us but living with it in the forefront of your life opens your eyes to the truth of it all, the inevitability of it all. Michael A. Singer has an interesting chapter on death in *The Untethered Soul.* He speaks of death as the great *cosmic paradox*…our best teacher. Death becomes the equalizer in body, wealth, power. The minute we are born, death is our shadow. We live with its certainty. Each breath we take could be our last and yet we deny, wasting so much of our lives oblivious…sleep walking…not realizing the minutia of our days *IS* our lives. I believe you saw this and struggled to live in the light—that you fought for the moments. Your jousts with death were many—a love/hate relationship—seeking and denying. There is no contest, of course. Death always wins.

April 6, 1984

….I still have flash backs and occasional obsessions w/ death and self destruction but more and more of my time is directed toward life. I even border on optimism at times. I do my positive verbal affirmations daily and I force myself to think and behave positively even when I don't really care or want to. I am determined to show all those who've helped me their time and love were not given in vain. I will grow and live and give back some of that time and love and the world will keep turning.

January 11, 1985, Friday, 9:30 PM (Visiting Gran in Florida)

I don't know if tonight is a point of victory or defeat or perhaps it is neither. Perhaps it is just another night in a string of nights wherein ecstasy has yielded to familiar doubt and discouragement. Tonight is different though and what I have to say can be found nowhere (to my best remembrance) in any of my years of journals. Perhaps it has been obvious but not to me. Even now I hedge and elude saying the words I detest even thinking. They are the most repulsive words to ever describe a condition. I would rather say, "I am stupid, or I am lazy or I am cruel, I am a sinner and I am a failure" for all of these have at their own time been true, but to say the words "I am sick" makes me want to vomit. "No!" I cry. "I am the healthiest person alive. I never get sick…never get sick…" but now today, I say to myself, in my heart and mind but to no one else, "I, LauraJo, am sick." I don't know what the hell is wrong with me. Sometimes I can't even care anymore because I've tried it all and the best has failed. And don't gimme the garbage about, not wanting to get better or needing my illness or tell me to take it to the Lord cuz I have and maybe I do and maybe I don't in reverse order. God strike me down right now if I haven't tried.

January 12, 1985, Saturday

I remember once coming home crying because of being teased and called a "thing" or "it" (not a boy and not a girl) because I carried a catcher's mitt to school. I wore shorts under my skirt. Ma told me not to cry or show anger when they shot spitballs in my hair on taunted me, because if I pretended not to care then they would stop. I know now in looking back that it must have hurt her very much to see me so lonely and hurt and she reached out to me with the best advice she had and Mom was right. It worked. They shoot a few spitballs, yell a few rude remarks and I would stare straight ahead and never flinch and they would get bored and bother someone else. She was right and it still works though I rarely need to… No, I never need it any more. No one much does that at this age. They just look at you funny or talk behind your back or never take an interest in the first place. Sometimes I wonder if that doesn't hurt even more than the spitballs.

January 13, 1985, Sunday, 7:30 PM

Two great nations…the Soviet Union and the United States, together we could probably solve the world's most pressing problems: famine, pollution, over population, painful and premature illnesses. I venture to guess that there is next to nothing that with combined effort we could not find a solution and yet we sit at long tables, our heads of government glaring unflinchingly at one another w/cynicism and fear……We live in fear of each other's power, afraid of the unknown advantage that will enable the other to make us their slaves. I guess I'm wondering one thing… Would we make them our slaves?

*It's time to stop asking **how** or **why** or **when** or **where**.? It's time to **do**, **live**, **shut up** and **get up**. It's time for a lot of things but then that old free will is not always my best friend or should I say that part of me is not always interested in the rest of me and what's best for the whole.*

I don't really think I am fighting w/God, but the arms talks in Geneva seem more productive and congenial That is really what it is like inside. I am different countries warring against myself, cynical, fearful and sure when I turn my back "they're" gonna get me!

.........I ran 29 min non-stop then swam another 30 min. Each step, each stroke kept time with sinful thought of self destruction, blood, death, pain and embarrassment to name but a few of the vivid but silent scenes. No positive pictures could overpower the seduction of misery, and what has become my personality held no grain of the past.

Ten years ago, there was no indecision, no fear of responsibility, no shame and self doubt. I doesn't matter where it came from, why, when, or how. That all doesn't make any damn difference. I used to think it could help to know. Maybe if I knew I could change back, regain my old strengths and virtues. Not so. It's only a distraction from growth today.

I get so sick of writing this shit over and over. You'd think I'd be bored to death w/it all, ready to can it and start fresh, try something different…I am so much more fed up then all those together who love me and they surely have had it!

I wonder where I am at just now. Admitting and accepting that perhaps like a paralysis I'll have to do my best w/it and quit the damn complaining (if only here in my journal.) Even that is too much. But I need this place, these pages whereon I write what I think and feel. They are my counselor. The one who sits and listens to all the crap I dump out. It is a lot cheaper than a shrink. A couple bucks will give me a place to turn every night for many weeks. And as I would toward a therapist I know I repeat the same lines over and over again but I keep writing because I must need to, and because now and then some new idea is born and if it takes a whole book for just one idea that's fine by me.

Since I don't know "why" I want to die, I do know "how". I want to bleed…that is why I choose rat poison. I want to see it running down my face and splashing on my hands and on the ground. It is such a pretty color red, blood is, and against the contrast of white skin the effect is awesome beauty.

I have refrained for a very long time though the urge has been strong at times. If only I had the nerve to hit an artery I could watch it hit the ceiling (so Mr. Tieppo at school says); that would be almost an orgasmic rush! Even picturing it is exciting. Most people don't understand but I do, and they don't matter really. I can get it all on my own w/out them. They do enhance it when they act appalled but my own witness is sufficient.

It is the watching of death that fascinates me. I squirt a spider w/Raid and watch it squirm for 45 minutes (feeling terribly guilty and awful the whole time for sure). So it is with myself. To jump off a building (tall enough) or blow my brains out would be too quick. There would be no time to witness the execution. Even with all of this I am not one to gawk at others misfortunes...not accidents or fires. I think it quite rude and obtrusive to do such human things. Sick... that's what it is. Sadistic and sick. I only ever did something like I said above to a spider because I am terribly afraid of them and keep my eye on them dead or alive just to make sure they are not going to get me. Sometimes I am sure if I turn my back they are going for the jugular. Silly, of course. Just a thought and everybody has crazy, silly absurd thoughts now and then that they never talk about.

Bowling today I saw a young boy, maybe 10 with his sister and parents, an alley to the left of us. He had some type of physical handicap and was trying his best to push the ball up the middle of the lane w/both hands. I didn't stare (most little kids bowl that way, his sister did too) but I check up on him now and then to see how he was doing. About 13 gutter balls later I looked over and found myself praying he'd get just one pin (one time the ball even stopped rolling before it got to the pins). He didn't look too sad or distraught, just kept plugging along in a quiet determined sort of way till out of the corner of my eye as I was throwing my own ball I saw at least 9 pins go down. It happened a lot more times into their next game and to his sister's loud verbal distress he even won that 2nd game.

I watched the parents watching their children. The mother, small and thin, chain smoked while observing from one of the ally's cold orange plastic chairs. Her son could have been a clone except for the sex difference. I noticed that (from her profile at least) she must have been a very pretty woman when she was younger but then I realized she wasn't that old. It was her eyes and the lines on her face that gave the impression of a difficult and trying life. Perhaps it had been only the past 10 or so years, maybe from the time a baby was born to her who the doctors said would not be like other children.

And now I think of Mom and Dad and these last ten years. How much has this aged them inside and out and did anything at all positive come from it or along w/it? I cannot undo any of it. Perhaps that is why I struggle so hard now to see and be a success today and tomorrow. The 4.0 I got last semester was for them. I needed so desperately to give them something, just one thing they could feel to be proud of me for. How could I say to them that they had not failed, that they had given me everything and more than I needed to make something of myself. Whether I do or not is not of them. How does a child make their parent understand that their love for the parents has nothing to do w/the love (or hate, author insert) I have for myself. To argue differently is to invite misunderstanding, confusion and pain. Then I would ask...who is the masochist?

I plead no innocence. Call it "no-contest" if you like. That best describes it. I throw myself on the mercy of the court and if there are no charges, I will go.

Well, my nails are gone (back down to stubs) I'm eating too much and sleep too much (too much is relative but over 3000 cals a day and 9 1/2 hours of sleep seems to fit). But I am learning something though w/some difficulty. I am learning how to keep my mouth shut and not argue... even when I know and have proof I am right! It actually feels great. It feels like I am really the one in control though I have not had the last word. I feel superior and I like that but I'll not say that and I'll try not to show it for to be humble is much wiser than to wear arrogance openly. I prefer sly arrogance, noticeable mostly to those who are arrogant themselves. "Takes one to know one!" so they say with truth. I wonder.

Chapter Thirty-two

May 6,1985, Monday, 11:45 AM

Is this the day to start a positive journal? Like most things, that's up to me. So what can I think of positive to say? Well, I suppose any event can be looked at from a variety of angles so I'll try to find the positive in what has been going on for the past few days. On Thursday, I went about helping myself rather indirectly, if not unconsciencously (sp?), calling Life-line unexpectedly and chatting for an hour (45 min about—stuff and only about 15 about rat poison). The last 15 min were the clincher to the police arriving at my door, though I had given no last name, phone #, or address. I've called so many times I guess they have me on file.

I overreacted a bit when the cops knocked on the door, climbing out the window and down the fire escape. One was on the front porch and we had a short foot race across the art galleries lawn. Some on-lookers must have thought I was a criminal because they headed me off but by that time I was exhausted and just sat down. There were about 3 cop cars and an ambulance in front of the house and they gave me the choice to either come voluntarily or involuntarily. I decided not to fight but to co-operate though I was a little upset. It was not "Life Lines" fault but my own. I had (for some reason) been honest and I told them I had eaten 75 bags of rat poison equaling about 7 lbs. I felt fine, really, and still do, but I knew I had hurt myself and it was wrong.

*The next few days were very difficult for me. I was angry and embarrassed and ashamed. I did not want treatment and refused it for a couple of days. They allowed me to do that which surprised me but was a relief too. I just didn't know what to do. It climaxed yesterday in the afternoon when I pressured myself to decide by turning in a pocket knife I'd had since I came in and by starting treatment. I created an uncomfortable incident w/ the knife but we all got through it and went forward. I received 6 units of plasma over about a four hour period, praying the whole time that I'd not get **"AIDS."** Dr. Carson has been away and though I know she'll be a bit disappointed I think it'll be OK and I'll not have to stay too long...especially now that I've accepted and received treatment. I've had to re-think my reasoning about some decisions. I want to change my mind but I also want to have some good reasons to do it. I can always figure out good reasons for what I'd like to try but Ma and Pa are right, as usual, when they say life is too short to waste making yourself miserable.*

I can work and play and dream and strive and I can do it far away or right here. But one place I can't do it is all alone. Sitting here on the edge of my hospital bed w/a constant companion and nice people all around, fixed up physically and w/a full stomach, it is easy to believe I can feel different, act different and make the positive changes I need to make. Believing that out in the world where I'm lonely and scared is the hard part.

May 7, 1985, Monday, 9:30 PM

Dr. Carson came by for a brief period a couple times and it went OK. She told me what the plan was and said she'd see me tomorrow. As she stood in the doorway to leave I wanted to go over and hug her but instead I remained at a distance, hesitation and questioning in my eyes. I don't know just what held me back but I was self conscience and felt distant and unworthy. "Distant" by choice, merited punishment for wrongs committed. I might have been afraid maybe she wouldn't let me or maybe she was secretly mad at me. Whatever the reason, I robbed myself.

The aid tonight has had similar problems as mine and we are able to talk fairly easily. We got to talking about change and how difficult it is and as I listened to myself, what I said sounded new…"Before one can change, self, as is, must be accepted."

Acceptance is a form of love and to endure the pain and scariness of change it takes sincere love (of self). It is so ironic. I really hate a number of things about me. My weight, my tendency to isolate, my petty intolerances. Sure, there is lots to change but I cannot hate Me because I hate some of the things about me…not if I ever want to change…so I just stopped and had a piece of cake after an aid who sat w/me a month ago said I was "getting fat." Nice, eh..?! Oh well, I am what I am. Would I be any different if she'd said, "My you've lost a lot of weight!" No. I'd just feel better… maybe, or I'd know she was lieing (which is more like it). It only matters how I feel about me and that's not too hot, but it will be better…I added that because I promised to be more positive.

Dr. Carson and I are going to meet at our scheduled time on Friday at 12:30. She says she still wants to meet the

Laura side of me. I said I'm always all here but Laura doesn't talk so she'll have to settle for me. Don't know what we'll talk about but it'll be so nice to be with her again for a little while.

Turn away when my tears come home
Please just look away when I cry.

Recognition belongs to those
Who will deny self pity's lie.

Find no room in your world for this.
Close the door tight and turn the key
Then follow the calling of life
Where enthusiasm is free.

Look to the sky but know the clouds
Have no power over your days.
A gentle rain can ease the pain
As well as the brightest sun rays

I've left room to finish my poem later. Starts out a bit down-beat but is picking up and has potential I think.

Came down to EW-2 at about 1:15. Put my bag in the wheel chair, broke the rules and walked. As long as I can do for myself I will choose to. I was up tight and reclusive for a while. Felt ashamed, like a failure that I was back so quick (even at all) but came out eventually and drew a new picture. Been thinking a long time about possible changes, new ideas and decided to get a bit more normal by being a bit more normal now so I called Mom. After about 8 times finally got thru and asked if they could both come see me. "Where? Ma asked and I said Genesee. No surprised response, only an "OK, we'll be there around 8:30."

Though I was nervous it went fine. Ma brought me some apple blossoms and she warmed up and was laughen and joking after a while. Dad stayed his usual quiet self. I told them the whole honest, grisly truth and then threw out my new ideas. We tossed them around for a while but then Jim came in about 9:45 and said they have to go now. They're coming back Friday so we can talk more about working for them and moving home. I truly believe it will work out fine. I can make it. They're so easy to get along with. I'll just have to work on not getting nutso about anything. The end is coming soon enough. I don't need to rush it............

............My feelings are hurt...Dr. Carson didn't come by today but I think seeing Ma made up for it some. I have really missed her...faults and all!

May 8,1985, Wednesday,12:30 PM

It happens so suddenly like choking on a piece of food, or a total eclipse viewed on time-lapse film and frozen in its darkest phase. I'm thrown into darkness by my own mind and heart w/out warning or cause and again I am left w/my fears...unknown fears.

All was well last night and up to now today. Plans were positive, energies high, but then, over a plate of chicken chow-mein I started thinking about my apt., my closet, the two hibachis and charcoal I have and the obsession returned in full force threatened by the fact that I've decided to quit living alone and move out of my apt. and back home for a while

2:15 P.M.

I just thought of what I get out of most of my self-destructive behavior. I get the thrill and fright of the very real possibility that I might die…and what do I get out of that? A sense of relief… but beings I don't want to die, what I do turns into mental and physical torture and I soon run out of answers to the "whys?"

Chapter Thirty-three

May 11, 1985, Saturday, 9:30 AM

I smashed my pencil sharpener last night and got the blade out. Guess I should have turned it in on my first inclination. I still can, or I could just throw the blade away...I could. I suppose I'm taking a chance writing this down in here but I don't think anyone is gonna read my journal and besides, it's up to me to turn it in or get rid of it. It's hid good. Mom brought in my box of little people and I have them on my window cell...sill. I wanted them because I know I'm going back to my apt. from here and I want to put them in my special trunk. There's days I doubt if I'll make it till the move home. Most days I'm sure I will, w/no sweat. I will, and it'll work out and I'll stop this stuff, break this pattern. The despair may persist but the behavior will change, so start now LJ...turn in the damn razor blade...start now. It's the only time you have to change is now. Do it NOW...No it doesn't need to be a symbolic "turn-in." Drop it down the radiator, do it for yourself NOW...NOW!

It only took a moment of time, a little fumbling to get it thru the opening and a wave of tears for the inner struggle. It was so simple and yet so hard, all at the same time and

*after the tiny sliver of metal was gone there was no ap-
plause, no "you done good" followed by pats on the back…
but there was a reward, a silent present of great value for
it seems that just briefly I was holding myself, soothing and
thanking me and in the silence I felt something akin to a
breeze on a stifling summers night, a moment of hope more
true than I'd felt for a very long time. True, because it was
subtle, not some hurricane sense of "everything is gonna
be fine," and I knew there will follow days when holding
myself will not be my choice, when I will hit and hurt again
because that weighs far more than the other side of the
scale at this point and maybe later I'll be pissed that I gave
into that good side. I probably will be, but right now I feel
like a tiny step has been made in the direction I must go to
survive, the only direction wherein I'll find true peace and it
was all for me, all for a silent reward and I cry now because
I'm so proud of myself, I'm grateful and I know it's the nic-
est thing I've done for me in a very long time. I actually
reached out and protected me…I said no to the assailant
and, who knows, maybe I've really started to climb out of
the pit. There is a good friend in me if I'll let her be.*

*One of the patients just came in my room and asked to buy
some of my sculptures. $5 or even $10 to $15 was her of-
fer but it wasn't the $. They are my original collection and
very special. After she kept at me I said I'd sell her the one
sort of up-beat one I had (the only one) because it was
slightly marred and I felt the head was oversized and out of
proportion but luckily, in time, I changed my mind and put it
back with the rest. So it isn't perfect, so what!? It was part
of my original 10 and they will remain a family and they will
go to live in my box w/the rest of my past and soon I will
rid myself of this past as I move onto an existence where
the gift of life is appreciated. It may take a long time, but
I'm only 28. It's only 10:30 and already I've performed an
act of self-protection and accepted a creation of my own*

that isn't perfect. It may be a gorgeous, warm, sunny day outside but the real beautiful day is taking place right in here behind these locked doors.

12:20 PM

Pam and I had a productive talk. I was able to break down my points that need work into three main categories, or perhaps I should label them "current problem areas," whatever...they are: (1) the despair (2) my self image and (3) my behavior. Number (1) may never change. It may be purely emotional or psychological. It may be physiological or, most likely, a combination of the three. I wonder still if it really matters. The important areas are those which can be changed and those are # (2, 3). Self image is a biggy. I think because it is so low is why I'm bad to me (maybe) but I'm working on improving it slowly but surely. That in turn will help me find another way to deal w/my despair.

Things like self-control, patience and stick-to-itness are great but they don't come naturally like we all wish at times. They take practice and every time they are exercised they become stronger until after a while there's not so much pain and effort needed to accomplish them. So I gotta quit thinking self control (for 1) should just come natural and start working on it. No matter how hard it is.

2:30 PM

How quickly my resolve faded. Eyeing the radiator, I visually dissected it, then right after one of the checks I proceeded to pull it apart. No luck, besides, I told myself I should leave the blade there. I lay back down. A couple

more checks (she was late) and I decided to give it a bet-
ter effort. This time I got it all the way apart. I'd taken off
one earring so, if by chance someone came in, I could
explain that I was looking for it. No one did and there in
the dust, along w/a few pills some prior patient had evi-
dently mouthed, was my precious razor blade. I grabbed it,
crammed it in my pocket and hurried at putting everything
back together. That was tougher than taking it apart but I
got it fixed OK. No one will ever know. Then I decided to
put a little makeup on and try to look halfway decent and
get out of my room for a while. I've been in here all day.
Right after I got it all together another check was made,
on time. It's amazing what one can accomplish in ten min-
utes. So the tug of war continues.

May 13,1985, Monday, 9:00 PM

Sunday was quite a day, an effort and a joy all in one, then
pain and frustration and ultimately, failure. I didn't write at
all yesterday because, for the first time, I was out social-
izing w/the other patients. I entertained a small group for
about 45 min. It was good for both of us. After that I just sat
w/a group of the rest of the patients and we talked about
nothing much at all, laughed some and just passed the
time. Ma showed up 20 min past visiting hours and stayed
for 10 min. I expressed my growing doubts about coming
home, how I didn't believe Dad was to gung-ho about the
idea. Around 10:30 I went to my room. I'd been guzzling
tea all day and was a bit high strung but that's just an ex-
cuse I made no more reasons to put it off and proceeded
to beat the hell out of my head on the window frame. Blood
got all over, on the window, on my hands, all down my
face, neck, It was great, a real mess, just what I guess
I wanted. After about 20 min I thought maybe I'd stop or
someone would come in--neither happened and though I

knew eventually someone would come, after about ½ hour I pushed the button and asked for a little help.

May 15,1985, Wednesday

Dr. Carson came by yesterday around 1:30 and told me they were shipping me to RPC (Rochester Psychiatric Center) soon. I was depressed before that but after, I couldn't quit crying all day. It must have been what I was wanting and I expect it was all because of the head-banging incident…

Now part of me just wants to run away but I know it's no answer and wouldn't help. There doesn't seem to be any tears left today. Yesterday saw a painful multitude and all not because I'll have to go to RPC but mostly because of what I've done w/and to my life up to this point…wanting to change…the tremendous amount of effort…most people say if you can't find the effort, then you really don't want it bad enough. So maybe they're right. Let them think I'm just a schmuck, or a bum or a jerk or all three. Thank God. He's my only judge and they're not.

My tears fell too for this lost summer which alone in anticipation has pulled me thru the long winter and soggy spring. The long warm windy days that can make even the most depressed feel OK about being alive. So I've robbed myself of one of the most precious times to me. Will this be punishment enough?

May 16,1985, Thursday

Burt came by yesterday and brought me a rose and told me he'd stick by me wherever they sent me. RPC looks inevitable...too self destructive for them to handle (at Genesee). So it's off to cockroach city where the patient-staff ratio is about 25-1.

2:30 PM (Rochester Psychiatric Center)

I have to guess at the time because they took my watch, my clothes, my necklace and all my other property, but I did finally, with quite s struggle, arrive at RPC. It's just about as bad as I imagined but thank God I'm fairly adapt-able. Right before they came w/the stretcher to get me, I was talking to Ma on the phone working up to asking her to bail me out again. No go. She said, not in a million years, I was on my own and I'd have to figure out how to get out... I'm still on one to one...but it's so sloppy here. Right now I'm sitting in a room all alone. Luckily I'm trustworthy at this point (luckily for me...I was so mad at Ma I hollered at her and practically broke the phone hanging it up... I fired Dr. Woltman and I'm pretty pissed at Dr. Carson. I couldn't give two shits if she ever sees me again and I don't want to see Mom and Dad again either...they don't care anymore so fuck them all... Burt just called. He cares, he even gave me a rose yesterday. It happens to be in a urinal because I couldn't have a glass vase, but it was still beautiful.

Oh well, at least I won't gain weight. The TV blares non-stop in the corner and we are all restricted to one large, relatively empty room. There are chairs, a couple small tables and a ping pong table w/no ball.

Some of the "crazy" folks I saw at Genesee beat me over here and are wandering about with the rest of them, un-shaven and sloppy in the hospital clothes provided to them, myself...included. They do not even let you keep your undergarments and I write w/a borrowed pen.

The staff ratio isn't quite as bad as I said but they all sit around at one table smoking and listening to their ghetto blaster drowning out the TV for the patients who are trying to watch that. Prison guards...no one-to-one patient assignment...minutes drag like hours. If I could get the window open, I'd jump it is so depressingly boring here.

Meds: I'm still on Vit. K and Phenobarbital w/valium as a PRN Q-4 I'm starting to rethink my decision about working for the family and living at home and school next fall. All three truly seem like my best bet. So what if Dad is going through his mid-life crises. It doesn't mean I have to take **it personally and as long as I know I'm not asking him to bail me out of anything then I'm fine. And about Ma not signing me out? Well, I guess that was for the best too. It'll help me feel like I alone really am at the helm of my life and that I can get out of my own mistakes and accept all my own consequences, not just the easier ones.*

Pain is so hard we always want it to end immediately, but then it is the only way to grow. I truly do believe that and though I wish all this would end, I know when it finally does, I'll be such a stronger, more secure, well rounded person and better ready to face the new pains that await us around each corner always with the many joys. I tell you Now--I'll be there!

Enough heavy stuff. How bout a little sick humor? I laid my head back and closed my eyes to meditate and this kid came over and said, "Do you always sleep with one eye open?" and I said that I had one glass eye and it did whatever it wanted, but everyday I'm feeling more and more like I'd rather wear a patch. I could get all colors w/lace and probably feel more comfortable.

*Where I get my feelings hurt is when I want to be con-
sidered special by certain people I care for. I want them
to like me and care for me just a little bit more than anyone else. I want to be special to them, not just different
but their favorite. It sounds like a little kid but I want them
"to like me best," and I guess it hurt my feelings when I
saw Dr. Carson on the floor with another patient one day
and she was being just as kind and caring and warm and
friendly and then she didn't even stop for a second to say
"hi" to me. Sure, I know I'm being silly, juvenile and imma-
ture. A kind person is a kind person, not just exclusively
to one person...ME. And when you're as busy as Dr. C
there's probably barely enough time to breath much less
say "hello" to every single one of your patients. OK, I can
rationalize it but, for some reason, it hurt and still does, to
know I'm not a little extra special. It teaches me that this
"specialness" must come from within, cuz if I don't feel it, it
won't matter if the whole world does; and vice versa.*

*When we are special to ourselves, no one can take that
away and the security goes beyond words. I don't think
too many people ever gain this level of self love, for though
it is far from egotistical, it is probably viewed that way by
many. I guess I wanted something from Dr. C, which she
really wasn't capable of giving. I have to realize she is not
my mother and that is one person who feels I'm very special but even in her life, Pat comes first.*

Guilty! Remember when you commented, LJ, about my lack
of *giving* my all to anyone...always holding back, and I agreed,
"That's how I've survived," I admitted. But you seemed to need
people's *all*. I'd become so frustrated with you because it (whatever it was) was never enough. You seem to need more than I could
give, or your friends, or your teacher, or in this case your doctor.
I know I am repeating myself, but the question is always there
and I have never understood why were you so *needy*? So many

friends stepped into your life: The Stephanies, the Suzannes, the Carries, the Dotties, more and closer friends than I, or most people ever have, and yet it was generally you who pulled away, fearful that they'd stop loving you and so you'd break it off.

You were wise in so many ways—in your head, but in your heart—the need, the void was huge, an ache that was always there. They, the infamous *they,* said it was a symptom of *Border Line Personality* Disorder, no self identity. Not identity, LJ, but self love. As imperfect as it was, love surrounded you with your brothers, your dad and me, and now as I read your journals, I understand that a lot of your frustration was that you were aware of our love. It was you who couldn't love you. Again, like in Oz, I think of you with a little, spoiled, angry, hurt child deep within you doing the cranking and the warning behind the curtain.

Chapter Thirty-four

Summer of '85: A month in Genesee Hospital and Rochester Psychiatric Center from still another overdose. Living at home, working with L&L, daily challenges. So what changed? Attitude?

July 17,1985, l:45 AM

...My meeting w/Dr. Pleune went well. I didn't have to swear on a stack of Bibles or anything like that. All I did was express my desire to try some medication and I ended up w/3 kinds: Lithium, Ritalin, and Meritel. That last one is a new anti-depressant on the market and since he got a big sample box he gave me some free. He was also very kind and only accepted $20 for the meeting...

July 18,1985, Thursday,12:30 AM

So far so good. Taking my pills just as I should and I think if anything is helping it is the Ritalin... It's odd how it doesn't really speed me up or make me anxious even though it is an amphetamine. Instead, it seems to help me stay on track more, to keep my day and my actions in line and headed in a positive direction. It helps my motivation level stay where I can do the things I have to do when I have to do them.

July 25,1985, 12:15 AM

I hope this is the last of these books I ever write (of this nature anyway). It'll be good when I move on and get too busy and too content to bother with them. Today was full w/work and teaching and sculpting. I'm contemplating be-coming a model (nude) for art classes. It pays between $6 and $8/hr for 3 hour classes. I am not embarrassed about my body anymore...it's pretty good as they go I think. ... Had a nice voice lesson w/Gwen (the model from class) we're going to trade voice for tennis lessons...

August 9,1985 Friday,10:30 PM

Still battling unreasonable fatigue...like one side effects of meds: cuts appetite. Don't like some of the others. Life is definitely a series of tradeoffs... Good tennis with Ma this AM. It's a good work out...playing better but get extremely tired in about 1/2 hour. Can't seem to shake the fatigue but it's there, tennis or no tennis. Spaced-out feeling is fading some.

August 12, 1985, 8:30 PM

The past few days I've been sick, the weekend, too tired and sick to even write, but it was a beautiful weekend weather-wise. Stopped my meds for two days. Fever (101)...just a virus? I swore I was on deaths door. It made me feel so sorry for people who are sick all the time...even wrote words for a song so I guess it wasn't all bad. Oh... got the job at Pizza Hut...I guess they'll get a tax break for hiring me because it is w/in 60 days (barely) of when I stopped SSI. It's too bad Mom can't. It doesn't seem fair that just because she's my Mom she's not allowed the same privilege of any other employer. It's very unfair, actually...

August 21, 1985, 11:15 PM

Not much time for writing these days...too busy living.

August 24, 1985, 11:30 PM

Went to party w/Ma tonight as Dad's sub. Volleyball and dinner at the Lays. Fantastic, fun time. Played 6 games. Talked w/Betsy's folks. Enjoyable.

Sept 9, 1985, Monday, 2:40 PM

Observation LJE: Dreams are goals unaccomplished, whereas goals are dreams in pursuit.

Though there are a few pages left, I am closing this journal because life has changed so drastically for the positive that I find myself needing to write much less and when I do, I want it to be in a book that is not tainted with overwhelming, depressive and morbid thoughts, ideas and recorded actions. It's time to start a fresh new, exciting and enthusiastic journal with, perhaps, fewer entries but of much higher quality. I'm out of the dark and into the light and I'm NEVER turning back again. Seven years in the tunnel was more than enough but it changed my life and made me a better person for which I praise God in thanks and wonder!

And we hoped that we had turned the corner and life was beginning for you.

September, 1985 at Granny's in Florida

Today was the best all day long practically. Sunned, sat by the pool, swam, ran, prayed, read, ate, went to see Hermann's Royal Lipizzaner stallions. Great…beautiful, bringing tears to my eyes, wonder and awe to my heart. No one could ask or be more thankful for such a glorious day. Then darkness fell, the sun was gone and anxiety, doubt and thoughts of suicide returned. I truly believed earlier in the day that I had it licked. They would never return this time for sure and especially without any instigating cause. Now what's worse, is I believe God can heal, cure…fix anything…but the catch is the person has to believe and desire healing. I'm stuck again with, It must be my own damn fault and/or desire.

So where do I go from here? Except up and down and up and always down. At the mall I saw a store (jewelry) w/Rolex watches in the window. Pam Rochow had one I admired and when she told me it was a Rolex I said, "That's nice" all the awe any pretty wristwatch deserves. Then today I checked out what this unusually pretty watch cost and it was close to $2000. What bothers me is that if I'd had the spare cash I would have bought it! That appalls me cuz I swore I'd never be like that and waste money that way when people were starving. Not me! I was not so vain or trivial. Surprise, LJ, you're a capitalist to the core. I wonder if I can be cured. I don't think it is very serious yet for it was only a thought, not a deed. Perhaps I've caught it soon enough. Time will tell now won't it.

A death penalty discussion between two ministers. The Baptist minister was all for it. The Lutheran was not. They both quoted the Bible to defend their positions. How interesting that the same book can defend such opposite points of view. Nuf said. Wanted to buy a hibachi today w/which to asphyxiate (sp?) myself in my car. Did not. Just a thought. Damn these obsessions. God told me to pray when they come to defeat them. Now it's up to me. As always.

April 29, 1986, Home in Rochester

…Dr. C just returned my call. I rung her back to save her the toll on the call and we talked a bit on trying to get below all the crap, to see beyond the smoke screen of pills and poison and get down to what is really my problem. She thinks it's got to do w/love and sexuality and my own sexual identity. Dr. Pleune agrees, so when I get up the courage to cut the crap and look at the real issues, then I may have a chance.

Your love and belief in Dr. Carson was unmatched in any of the doctors who worked with you. She was the only doctor that you allowed to use hypnotism. The results? "I was afraid I could not put her together again!" Dr. Carson's words.

May 2, 1986

…I wanted to ask Mom today point-blank that if the pain just became too great, would it be acceptable if I ended it (my life) right here at home in my room or should I go off alone by myself? I couldn't ask. I didn't want to worry, scare or offend her…plus I didn't have the nerve. Besides, things are getting better and I probably wouldn't even think of it… especially after more time goes by and my spirits rise.

In quiet moments, I have wondered if I could, if I found you in a coma just hold you and let you go. How frightening and lonely it must have been for you and all those who suffer as you did, to be alone. Although I've read we all die alone, I do not believe that. Those who cannot be with their loved ones in the last moments of life on this earth have difficulty accepting the departure of their loved one's soul. Saying "good-bye", holding our loved ones hands and wishing them *safe journey* connects the soul of those left behind with those departing, and I believe love lessens the fear for both individuals. One of my greatest sorrows is not to have shared this moment with you.

Chapter Thirty-five

In The Dark

All alone in the dark at night
I could lie down w/out a fight
And let my life just slip away
Before the dawning of the day.
I do not know reality
From monsters in the dark I see
For they are real, as "real" can be
And though ashamed, they frighten me.
Come morning all my tears are dry
And I can see it was a lie.
There is no need to run and hide
From all those fears I hold inside.
So as the wind picks up at dawn
I'll see them go and they'll be gone
Beyond my vision they will fade
Yet for their death, I have not paid.

May 5, 1986, Monday

**Observation LJE: There is no practice In dying.
Even in sleep there are dreams.**

Somehow, with the morning light, I'm not so frightened anymore. I'm almost glad Dr. Carson didn't return my calls so that I could feel, just maybe, I handled it on my own and that I'm more capable than I give myself credit. A big part of me believes it's the meds that helped, as I've been trying to take them regularly as prescribed for the past couple weeks. The literature says it can take up to 4 weeks for them to help and I think it's been almost 3. I've never really focused on myself as a fearful and phobic person but that's what Nardil is supposed to be especially helpful for. Agoraphobics. I'm not an agoraphobic but, if it came right down to it, I guess I'm a life-a-phobic and that's the worst fear of all. Regardless if, how, or why, I do believe they may be helping so I'm gonna keep taking them along w/ the lithium in an effort to make it thru this hard time without a hospitalization or another screw up. This morning it feels possible and I'm gonna try and hang on to that feeling. Lord knows how rare it is but I know how great it is.

May 7, 1986 (HomeArama in Victor)

Seems like a lot has happened since Monday. Maybe it's more inside than out though. I went over to paint a tree yesterday, a very damaged, injured tree that didn't look like it had to good a chance at survival. At first it was just a messy, tedious, rather distasteful job that I preferred to finish than start but as I painted and climbed, caressed and doctored this poor tree, I began to feel involved personally with its well-being. It began to matter very much to me that this tree make it and suddenly I noticed I was crying and if there was a special God for trees I was praying to Him with the most sincere wish for this tree's health as I had prayed for anyone's health, tree or person. A man drove by in his truck and shouted out to me, "20 bucks it doesn't make it to the show...!" I looked up at the tree then I looked at him and all I said was, "There's always a miracle." And for this tree it may take just that but then, it has Ma on its side and if any person ever had a near magical green thumb it's Ma. That tree couldn't have a better friend coupled with the fact that I smeared nearly 2 lbs of tar on its open wounds (only a few blobs on me) and Ma trimmed it and watered it and tied it down good. We shall see what we shall see.

(That tree lived for years, LJ. You did good!)

May 8, 1986

Saw Dr. Pleune. He is an interesting man that's for sure. Pretty open minded and talk about original ideas...well, I'll not go into it, but if I run out of ideas on how to be masochistic or how to kill myself, Gordon could entertain me w/a few. That's what I like about him; he doesn't try to prevent my stupid acts or be my savior. He does tell me I'd be better off if I rerouted my energies into more constructive areas and once he said "Why don't you just cut it out and be a little nicer to your body?" But then I could tell he knew that approach was no good so he took another, like suggesting more dramatic way of dying like Anorexia Nervosa. I laughed and said I loved food too much, but speaking of food it's just about exactly 6 weeks till my birthday and I started my diet today, the 500 cal or less diet. Today was a success...No sugar, lots of lettuce and a couple of carrots and ½ a cuke. Of course, I don't know how many calories were in the ¼ cup rat poison powder. That probably won't be a regular part of the diet anyway......tastes too disgusting. Today I mixed it (rat poison) w/Crystal Lite drink mix but I think it'd be better w/chicken bouillon or hot chocolate.

May 9, 1986

...Right now I'm waiting for my chicken bouillon to cool so I can add that green disgusting stuff and see if I can drink it w/out barfing. I'm sitting here screaming at myself "why?" Chicken bouillon was far too salty and very unstomachable...I decided to try Coke next but that was like dumping root beer on ice cream from about a foot above the glass. Total fuzz, and believe me, rat fuzzy is not very good. You can hardly taste the coke and foam is hard to swallow. As it is, I waste 1/3 to 1/2 of every batch I mix up...I'm going to try chocolate milk next. First I mixed up some sugar free hot cocoa and put it in the fridge to cool, then I'll mix that w/ some skim milk. That way it'll be as low cal as possible. I still wish I knew how many calories were in a bag of that stuff....

I was bad on my diet, still just had fruit and veggies and meat (oh and rat poison) but no sugar...

Maybe I'm going about it all wrong, trying to drink it. Maybe I should mix it with spaghetti sauce into a paste and just eat it...just a thought.

May 9, 1986, 11:30 PM

Chocolate milk is by far the winner so far...

Dr. Carson loaned me a book about this little girl who is so cute and quick and everyone loves her. To know her is to love her and I can't stomach it...jealous I suppose. Just cuz I was a little kid no one could stand, who always said stupid stuff and got into trouble...well I don't know why it irritates me to read about some little kid who everyone loves and want to have around and thinks is so adorable and precious...maybe I could learn something even now. It would probably be very educational for me to read, but I'd rather eat rat poison... Good night!

May 10, 1986 (HomeArama)

Taking my meds right on schedule and in the proper amounts, hanging in there on my diet of no sugar and today I've been working all day washing windows and cleaning. We do the windows w/newspaper and ammonia and water. Occasionally I glance at a piece in the paper I'm wiping with and read about the tragic death of some heroic wonderful person like this lady who had some rare disease from birth but was real brave and praise worthy about it all. Her unusual courage made her someone extra special when she died. Since she was so wonderful this world is a bit lesser place w/out her and we should all cry just a bit more than when John Doe down the street who never accomplished anything dies. He never exhibited great courage or noteworthy talents. In fact, he drank a bit too much and for a time was on welfare. But what no one knows is just how much John Doe (or maybe it was Jane Doe) suffered during their lives. None of us walked in their shoes or cried their tears. We'll never know how hard they tried and how much they suffered because it never seemed hard enough... I...picked up the spaghetti sauce and some diet pudding mix to try a new mixture... Looks like Granny has diabetes. Take a lesson, Look what too much sugar can do!

10:00 PM

Really a great day. Sunny and about 70° We picked up pine needles, went to work at Century 21 to untangle some mortgage mess…got home…Ma talked me into going on a bike ride. It was really good…reminded me of camping days years ago. Traveler came the whole way too, he's an energetic old dog.

It won't mix w/spaghetti sauce, turns into red glue. Uck! A red glue w/green flecks and a terrible flavor…back to chocolate milk but even that doesn't work too well, not thick enough to suspend the particles like the ice cream (that's what I used before) but I'm on a serious diet and ice cream just isn't acceptable! The milk is too thin and I barf up half of it…Capsules would work but…too expensive. It's already cost me nearly $60 so I won't get those leather boots I'd been eyeing or…

*Life is a struggle for everyone…whether they have a rare disease, live in a wheel chair, or write famous stories and books. And in the same right everyone is worthy of acclaim and praise for the job they did because I truly believe **most all of us do the very best we can.***

May 14, 1986, Wednesday, 9:30 PM

The pain last night was so bad I didn't sleep at all. The heating pad on my stomach helped some. You'd figure w/ that I'd quit and part of me did. Part of me asked Cecile for some Vit. K but the other part doubled my intake so that now it's worse than it ever was before. I got blood coming out just about everywhere and the pain is getting worse. Dr. C is going to call in a prescription for Vit K for me tomorrow but I wonder if I'll take it. Maybe if it hurts bad enough tonight I will…

May 15, 1986, Thursday, 8:00 AM

How do you tell someone you love and who loves you that the terrible shape you are in is self inflicted? What are they supposed to be except angry and affronted? How do you explain something you don't understand yourself and how can you ever expect understanding in return. The pain was equal if not worse last night and my pee is blood red. Still, my gums aren't bleeding and neither are my eyes so it's been worse…

June 1, 1986, Sunday, 8:30 PM

Pages have been torn out and all the old has been put away and set aside. The numbering system has changed and this journal shall be listed as #1 AD. AD stands for "after death" for on Thursday, May 15th, a little more than two weeks ago, I was told that I died from the rat poison and Tricyclic overdose I'd taken. It was odd because I hadn't really meant to die. I even took a quarter with me to the rest area so I could call for the ambulance if I got scared which I was sure I would, and I did, but it was almost too late. In fact it was too late. I was vomiting blood and unconscious by the time they arrived. And by the time we reached the hospital I'd gone into violent seizures and almost bit my tongue off. Shortly thereafter I quit breathing and then was void of any pupil response to light. Dr. Carson said that meant damage to the brain stem and little-to-no chance for recovery, especially a full recovery w/no serious brain damage. Dr. Carson said essentially I was dead, gone, veged out, hopeless...but outside that place people were still hoping and not only that, they were praying. Ann Welch said she prayed til 4:30 in the morning Friday the 16th and later got a call from an important California business man, a friend from years past who had felt an overwhelming urge to leave his meeting and pray for her because he'd been given the sense that she was "fighting for her life" and the prayers continued, literally from coast to coast until w/ out explanation I started to breathe again and my eyes started to work again or should I say my brain did and with tremendous effort, tears and pain I was back again. I remember opening my eyes on the 3rd day down in ICU and the first person I saw was Dr. Carson. I tried to smile though I felt ashamed and I said in surprised gratitude... "You came."

She smiled back, a bit tired and said, "This is about the 3rd time I've been here." Then I saw Kurt later on and he revealed the same truth. He'd been to visit a couple other times too...but I wasn't home.

There is no memory of being gone, no great revelation nor witnessing of a bright light and wonderful feeling of peace. It was just dark and quiet w/no thoughts, no dreams. Just nothing and then I started to wake up to someone yelling at me to "open my eyes" and telling me I had a tube down my throat to help me breath.

One plus about this time was that when they extubated me, which is a horrible experience, I was still so out-of-it that I didn't notice fully the pain. Mostly I just noticed that for a while I couldn't talk and then later I could but there was this awful pain in my mouth. In order to try to save my tongue, the ambulance people had shoved a bite-stick in my mouth and ended up cracking my front tooth way up high. Then when they got my mouth open and put a block in, I chomped down on it so hard that I cut a deep gash through the roof of my mouth almost to the bone. That along w/a row of teeth marks cut along the side of my tongue, eating was next to impossible so I ended up losing 14-15 lbs, half of which I've gained back already. I've never been so totally wiped out after a self-destructive act. All I did for nearly 5 days was sleep. Lucky for that because there was nothing to do and no one to talk to on four and if it weren't for Dr. Carson coming up for a few minutes every day I'd have been emotionally totaled.

Tubes and needles, humiliation and pain. From emergency to ICU for 3 days then up to the 4th floor for 5 days. Blood transfusions, shots, charcoal, extubation and an endless stream of pills until soon I was nearly well enough to leave. But where was I going? That was the scary part.

I was initially scared but Dr. Carson assured me I would not be going to RPC (State) and that depending on how my time on 4 went, I may be able to go straight home which was what I did on Friday, May 23rd. Dad came in to get me and we met w/Dr. C. for a while on Dad's request for him to express his feeling on how what I did and have done before, affects him. I think it was helpful to him and I got a lot out of it too. So 9 days from start to finish took me from life to death and back to life again. I was still exhausted and Dr. C. told me to take it easy for at least 2 weeks.

I did not go visit you this time, LJ. I couldn't watch it all over. I met Dr. Carson in the emergency and we talked, but I couldn't stay—too many times hovering over your bed watching you struggle. There comes a time in each of our lives when self pres- ervation steps forward and that voice inside screams, "No More!" We didn't talk about it when you came home, just tried to pick up life with the usual, mundane chores.

June 3, 1986, Tuesday, 9:00 PM

Well two weeks ended up being about 2 days and with all we had to do there was no avoiding a full schedule once again. It was OK though because I really was feeling much better.

Since then much has happened. A new church, a new (used) motorcycle and lots of work to be caught up on (not new). But all this is for later, it's bedtime now.

"Don't bring her back." That's what Ma told me she said to Dr. Carson when it looked so bad. Ma felt I'd gone through the worst of it and it would be cruel torture to jerk me back from where it appeared I wanted to be any- way...dead. I guess they just can't take it anymore and I can't blame them for wishing it would stop, however it had to stop. Even so, I know they still love me and I'm pretty sure they're glad I'm still here... Personally, I can't stand it anymore either. It's eating me apart inside and out and there is no where left to turn. I continue to take my Lithium and Nardil as prescribed. Exhaustion comes easy and my throat is still killing me......Dr. C is ceasing her internal medicine practice... It's a scary thought...she's done so much for me...this past crises must have been terribly difficult for her because I know she loves me a lot as I love her too. She had to make a lot of very difficult decisions and take on a lot of respon- sibility. I'm surprised she can still find it in her to care about me at all...

June 13, 1986, Friday, 10:30 PM

Lots has been happening, lots of good stuff. I decided to quit being such a hypocrite today and I dumped out my bottle of Tricyclics. there was enough there to do the job right and there was also enough there to send a twinge of shame thru me every time I claimed to "Trust in the Lord." But now they are gone and while it is a relief, it is also a loss of a sort and there is just the whisper of regret at their disposal. Now I suppose I shall have to keep my promise to live life and surrender the "terminal" option. Life can never be fully lived nor enjoyed while clinging to the option of self destruction should the pain get too bad. Joining the human race is scary.

June 24, 1986, Tuesday, 8:30 PM

Observation LJE: Time can only be wasted when it is held of value.

.....I've slipped back into lying on my bed and dying. Yet fight its practicalities and realization of what the end would mean to my best understanding...no more sunsets, no more moon rise, no more glistening silver thaws on cold winter morn, no more holidays or birthdays or baby showers or wakes for there is no birth w/out death. No more bird songs or summer rains, thunderstorms or blizzards.

No more swaying in the breeze at the top of a cherry tree, or gorging myself w/strawberries in the field, no more racing on my motorcycle with the wind in my face and the sun hot on my back toward a beach were my family awaits... no more family or friends, no more laughter or tears no more anything at all...and then I roll over struggling to turn

*off the death thoughts, grab a funny book, walk to the win-
dow and see the sun going down once more. Why am I
so tired, weary with my gifted and blessed world so often?
Counting my blessing daily is of no avail..."Self apprecia-
tion" isn't even all that great these days either, it's just too
much work. I get tired before I get anywhere near a climax.
I swear my hand is gonna fall off before anything happens.
Why bother? I hate being so different. I'm so afraid of love
and closeness and sexual touching. I can't even be gay!
Oh, yea, I did go to 8:00 church where we're studying Job
still. Talk about suffering! My life's a bowl of cherries in
comparison...except inside.*

July 2, 1986, Midnight

*Molly (can't get used to calling her that after a month of
calling her Moe) and I had a softball game tonight out in
the middle of No-Where's Ville. It was loads of fun as usual
and we even won. I used my new mitt. Made a great catch
(knocking down another fielder in the process) and had a
good solid base hit... We stopped at Wegmans on the way
home....I realized I'd locked my keys in the car. Everyone
was so helpful, the staff inside, passing customers and
finally a fellow went and got a State Trooper to help me.
Molly got a ride home with a friend... I stood in a down
pour while the very kind police officer struggled to open
the door... Finally...he triumphantly and gallantly stepped
aside handing me the set of keys that was on the floor...
I just thanked him, Said God bless and gave him a hug
(after asking if I could). Then, in embarrassment I crawled
into the car dripping wet, set Molly's set of keys on the seat
and pulled my own out of my pocket which I just found as
I climbed in. There was no way I was going to tell anyone*

I had not only been so stupid as to lock my keys in my car, I'd been stupid enough to have them in my pocket all the time! That was unbearable and as far as I'm concerned the secret will die w/me.

Chapter Thirty-six

As the years passed, we began to recognize the signs as you slipped back into your abyss: huge sugar consumption, energy drop, more reclusive. When the curtain began to close, we knew that the evil blackness was enveloping you again.

How many times could you work your way back to the light? Was there another possibility that we had overlooked? Did the answer lie within us, the genetics of unknown generations? Were you born to suffer? Was there no choice? Had we tried hard enough? Unlike some families, insurance dollars were available. As the years went by and avenue after avenue proved to be a dead end, we began to see your hope and courage dim. Anger? You placed no blame, encouraged *us* to get *help*. My search is nearing an end and yet there is no answer, no "Ahhaa." I still ask, "What was the point?"

I thought I had reached a point of acceptance, but deep down I denied the possibility that you would give up so I discounted your words on that last Christmas, "I think I can go now…you and Dad will be OK."

My silence to your words was not indifference, not the shield of denial, but disbelief. Although there were times, especially that last time when I realized, when I knew that it would happen again and again, when I told Dr. Carson to let you go…it was not a matter of what I wanted…it was for you.

Friday, Nov. 7, 1986, 6:30 PM

I try to think of why I don't sculpt anymore or sing w/my guitar and write poems to put to music.

In part, it just seems like it's not there anymore. Like what was once a raging river of emotion seething to be poured out has dried to an unnoticeable trickle shrouded by a dark cloud of negativism.

My very work shows it. One of my last contracted pieces was turned down because it lacked the proper, if any, emotion and then this last one I tried even though I poured myself into it, ended up cold and heartless (so-to-say) and without any, by my interpretation, redeeming characteristics. The songs won't flow, the words won't rhyme and it's embarrassing to say I guess I just lost the energy and desire to even try so the kiln sits collecting cob webs as the dust piles upon an abandoned guitar case and whatever creativity there once was in me has taken on a dormancy not unlike an appearance of death. It seems a bit barren to drive it as far down as the word "death" does but I can't help say how it feels. I see no resurrection of creation in statue or song.

But somewhere deep down, like all of us who believe in a surviving goodness within, I know it's there waiting for me to come get it, to nudge it from a self-assigned sleep and shake it to a full awakening of all the glorious things we can be together......

November 10, 1986, Monday, 11:30 PM

It's so frustrating how old habits never seem to change and how they begin to take over our lives. Even the method of attempting to break the undesirable habit becomes a habit. So it is and continues to be w/me. I sit and make my little calendars, draw in the little boxes, marking each with a #. Day #1 being the magical day when I simply cease my old annoying imperfection and day "last" being the mark wherein I've attained that perfection so long sought after. POOF, just like magic almost 30 years of doing something a certain way is changed and all because I made this little chart w/its lines and #'s and boxes. If ever I begin to believe I'm even halfway intelligent I'll simply remember this ritual, the countless failures and try not to waste my time doing it again. But for now I'll look for the magic day "1" and the perfection on day "last" Hope springs eternal—right!?

November 12, 1986, Wednesday, 11:15 PM

Well, I know I'm no bible scholar but I think that the bible says to hate or think poorly of one's fellow man is to harbor the same contempt for God. We shall be judged as we judge and this being the case I'm in big trouble. On one hand, I'm thinking I should hang around till my attitude changes and becomes more loving and forgiving. On the other hand, I can't believe my attitude will ever change and if God is like people, I don't want to go spend forever w/ Him. I know He created us all and so there's at least something special in everyone cuz of that but sometimes that spec of God in a person is so small it's invisible. My spec isn't much bigger than invisible and perhaps it's smaller cuz I know how I should be and am not. More blame there than in ignorance I suppose, and still I am torn over what I do not know but long to believe in my heart

All things, events, places, ages, and times are NOW. God just breaks them up into totally separate experiences because our little minds and hearts couldn't take such a humungus existence all in one blow. I am born, living, old and dieing all in this instant. This step I take reaches into every realm I'll ever know or have known and all in this moment and breath. Cept my little pea brain gets stuck on the pain, smiles at the beauty, cries in the rain and reasons that because it's so hard sometime I've got to leave, that I really won't be able to stand it any longer.

Should I, in a moment of rash contempt for humanity, end my short stay here, then I shall certainly cry out for an eternity over such a foolish mistake. Should God grant me peaceful rest, then it would be a blessing beyond all heavenly generosity. Already in life I've gotten many good things not deserved or worked for: my family, my health, my talents and hardly last, the love of total strangers who have been there to care for me when all seemed lost and irreparable.

How can people hurt so much or seem so disgusting with all that I've had? The years have honestly mellowed me out a bit. I'm daring to think I've finally grown out of all of it.

Thinking about the future and making plans is a definite sign of a new Maybe-I'll-hang-around-attitude. Maybe I'll never amount to anything gr eat, but if I just learn to be… that'll be great.

NORMAL

"Normal" tell me what it is.
Tell me what I am not.
Do not count my years
Assuming where and what should be
I may not be "normal"
But I am me.

Choices

Chapter Thirty-seven

"Little Roo," the love of your life. Remember how you scoffed at Granny when she cooked special dinners for Snookie, her dog. For your birthday, we gave you $100 with the stipulation that you must spend it on a dog...better than any psychiatrist we had read. Having always been an animal lover, we had dogs...always rescued...there was Cricket, a small wiry Welch terrier, Traveler, part beagle, Fred, well, we couldn't figure out what Fred was besides a *get-even* dog. Chewed up Granny's wicker basket, ate the forsythia bush we tied him to, ruined the rug trying to dig out of the basement, went through how many screens, and on and on. When your father asked, in exasperation, "What do you see in that damn dog?" I pointed out to him Fred's greeting: his flip, flops, pants, kisses, roll overs in his joy to see me.

"Do you do that when I walk in?" I asked. And that's what we wanted for you. The total love—unconditional—that a dog lavishes on his master.

How can I describe the joy you had in Little Roo, another rescue dog. Breed? No idea, it didn't matter. You followed Granny's ways...into the kitchen concocting special dinners. He went everywhere with you. Those ears! We thought he must be part rabbit. You used to tie a bandanna around his head, tuck him into your leather jacket and ride with the wind on your motorcycle.

And then the unthinkable happened. We were completing Shielie's house next door. November–so many vehicles in the drive as there always are when it came to house closings, vehicles always having to be moved. You volunteered, not aware of Roo and Fred running around playing in the yard. You hardly even felt the bump. I knew! You would not survive Roo's death.

Friday, November 14, 1986, 10:45 PM

(No other day in my life has born such sorrow) Little Roo, forgive me. I'm sorry, I love you.

I held her in my arms and rocked her every day since I first picked her up September 3rd. I smoothed her soft white hair with my cheeks and complained...not too earnestly... as she crawled up my chest and perched herself on my shoulder to keep watch while I drove and then rounding each corner I'd reach up and hold her steady so she wouldn't fall. She was so tiny but so brave. She'd climb open-back stairs just to be up where I was sweeping and she'd crawl out of her little basket to sit up high on the handle bars on my bike and when it got cold she'd let me put a little bandana over her ears to keep her warm. She'd look like a little old granny but oooh I was such a proud beaming mama when everyone who saw her went bonkers over her. That very first night she slept right in my hand and after that, right next to my pillow. Roo had such a spirit, fearless, curious, loving and forgiving. She was smart as a whip and so happy and playful. Everyone loved her dearly, but today at 3:00, I was moving one of the subs vans and crushed her between the rear wheel and a rock. I heard her cries and by the time I was out of the van, Jeff had her in his arms. We rushed her to the animal hospital where they did everything possible for her but she died on the table from massive internal injuries.

I killed her, my little Roo, my precious and only friend, the apple of my eye and one of my very strong reasons for being. God it hurts. Nothing has ever hurt me this much inside. The power of my grief is beyond words and the tears will not cease. I sit in the cold deserted garage screaming my sorrow into the dark of night and then suddenly it was dark not only outside but in too. A fuse had blown and for no apparent reason except for the overloading release of all my pain.

There is nowhere to run, no place to hide, no one to call to make it all better. I've prayed and prayed for peace and understanding but all I still possess is my pain, grief and unimaginable loss. I loved Roo w/as much love as I've ever given to anyone. Now at age 29 my heart is broken for the first time from a loved one's death. Learn LJ.

Nov 15,1986, Saturday, 9:00 PM

Until yesterday I thought I knew what nearly unbearable pain was but now I find it can, will, and does, even now, get much, much worse. I thought I knew what a broken heart felt like but to this, everything and every hurt before was merely a webbing of hairline fractures. For it is now that I know my heart is truly beyond repair…

All that are left are memories, a little strand of hair on a pillow, a vision of her lying by the fire chewing on any free toe that may have passed by and running rings around herself in hot pursuit of her tail…

Ma cried nearly as many tears as I did yesterday and came home w/a little puppy to console me and get me something to give all this love to. But let's face it, one hour after Roo's death was just too soon…

I rushed to the pet store—desperate. A fruitless attempt to hold death at bay. Of course, it was the wrong thing to do. I felt the pain in my heart and knew how magnified it must be in yours. I had to do something! I didn't hear your wailing. I didn't hold you and wail with you! Why? I didn't know how. I've always gone into my cave, licked my wounds, worked out my pain. I thought you needed the same stage, the chance to come to grips with the horror of your part in Roo's death, so I forced myself not to hover.

But you needed the warmth and comforting of understanding arms as most folks do. I knew I did not have the words, but little did I know that when there are no words, there is the physical embrace of understanding, of the sharing of grief that can lessen the torment.

We never spoke of your horror. I waited for you to share your grief. You never did and I watched you suffer. Helpless to stop it.

November 16, 1986, Sunday, 5:00 PM

Ma just reprimanded me for being so sullen. She says, "You can be glad for what you had and go on or you can mourn and mourn." I looked at her and snapped, "I'm going on."

What right has she to tell me how long I can and cannot grieve. Well I hope she takes her own great advice after

I've gone to look for Roo. I hope she just feels deliriously happy for what she had then goes on and doesn't mourn more than a moment or two. That's all I'm worth. Roo's worth much, much more. How dare she tell me how to handle my grief, assuming she knows its depths and intensity? How dare she be so presumptuous! It's probably simply because she wants to forget and go on but can't when she sees me moping around. We're all just being selfish.

Selfish? I can't believe this entry...that I'd be so calloused. I look at the date. How could I expect anything but grief from a love as great as what you felt for Roo? That you were filled with such pain, her death magnified because of your part in it...the horror of it all was almost too much for me, what could I expect of you?. Deny? It was my inability to comfort, to absorb the shock and pain, to protect you. No! I wouldn't let it happen...look forward, not back... but I knew what would be the result of this tragedy. Could I ward it off by shutting the door to the event, pushing you to look ahead?

I want to hold little Roo just one more time but Dr. Lill says I should not. I have no pictures of her, only what my memory holds and those I know will fade w/time. Lord, I don't want to forget her, not any little part of her. I always want to be able to call her beautiful face to mind.

Looking back over these years, I see myself constantly w/my foot in my mouth, judging others ass-uming I know where they're coming from. What a horrible lie I've believed, because now as others judge my reaction to this loss I am hurt and angry at their audacity. They have no right—just as I was wrong so are they. Each person's grief, mourning and pain is an individual snowflake of suffering. How can I say they are wrong.

LJ and Little Roo

November 17, 1986, Monday, 1:30 AM

Little Roo gave me a sculpture tonight w/all the old feeling I used to put into them. I put together a box of all her belongings: her ball that she used to carry around by the fuzz, her little yellow rubber tug toy that she and Traveler used to play with, her collar, her dish, brush, vitamins... I will fire them with my sculpture of me clutching this limp form of Roo, which I never really got to do. The piece sits on a rock and in the rock are two holes, a little one for her and a bigger one...

Chapter Thirty-eight

November 22, 1986

Sometimes it's as if I'm two people at once. Part of me sits rocking back and forth cross-legged on the floor, crying and sobbing that she wants to stay here, that death is too final and scary and life really isn't all that bad, its actually pretty good and I want to see more, experience more, know more…pain or no pain, happiness, a home. It's worth it to stay and I'll fight anyone who tries to make me leave, and then out pops Laura saying I'm no good, life's no good. It sucks and it always will. I'll always hurt and feel lonely inside. It's time to go now, not tomorrow… quit putting it off. You know you want to die anyway; this is just a spanking for your own good.

Then I argue, but it hurts too much, physically, emotionally and also my integrity suffers a shameful blow. They take you where people hate you for what you've done, where people can't begin to have the slightest bit of empathy or understanding. You're just an asshole in their eyes and that's hard to take too. I don't want their sympathy or even empathy but I don't deserve their disgust either. When have they walked in my shoes? Lord, I have it so good please help me not to throw it all away. I know I have free will but I need your help cuz my free will is all whacked out. I'm believing those lies Satan is bombarding me w/moment by moment. Lies that I know are lies, but are so tempting to believe. God, you've helped me countless times already in my life. I've probably used up my quota, but if you can see fit to bail me out, see me through, help me choose right one more time, well then I think my chances will be super for making this life of mine work and work to your glory.

November 27, 1986, 6:15 PM

............I still can't believe that happened (another OD)... I felt sicker than I have in a long time plus my teeth feel like I've cracked them all in two...Ma, with her 6th sense, called a couple times. I reassured her, told her it was purely accidental, that I had switched meds hoping to feel better but it had backfired. I told her about my new puppy "Billy" and she seemed pleased. Billy's a cotton ball, a girl and a real cuddler.

I was surprised and pleased when you came home with a new puppy, a little white ball of fluff you named Billy Jean (BJ) after your tennis idol. I had chewed on my mistake with the puppy at Roo's death. I waited. I knew that you could love again, but would you survive the grieving? "She's a miniature Samoyed, Mom. They were asking $25 for her, but they were so poor, living in a trailer, so I gave them $30."

Billy Jean

December 17, 1986, 7:00 PM

Billy no longer looks like a big round cotton ball…more like a cotton ball with 4 stick legs and a red bandanna about its neck. She wears Roo's old collar and handkerchief (sp?) and I swear sometimes Roo is living inside there w/her. Billy is awfully cute. Still peeing on the floor at will…but I suppose it's still forgivable at 9 ½ weeks of age.

Called Dr. C's answering machine, stressed but it was no emergency. I've promised to make it thru Christmas…finally other people's cigarette smoke has become a bone of contention. Drs. say yes, smokers and cigarette manufacturers say no. They scream that to make smoking in public illegal would be constricting their freedom. Well, I say "my" right to clean air, which is a necessity to health and life outweighs their right to freely pollute my air or should I more correctly say "our" air. It seems too clear, so obviously cut and dried but those smokers just won't stop blowing their fucking smoke into my lungs. Talk about selfish jerks...oh why do I do this to myself? Get all worked up over something that will not be changed...at least not in my life time.

I know I do rude, selfish things from time to time but when it comes to poisoning a human life, at least I limit that action to self alone and don't go about violating others' lungs, clothing, food and eye sight with a stinking, lousy selfish cigarette. I'd like to tell them all where they can stick their butts and hopefully they'd be lit when they do! How's that for a convincing scenario for an unforgiving, rigid, unsympathetic, or empathetic critical bitch? Not bad eh??? Well that's how I feel about it all and people probably hate me for just about as good a reason. So like it always ends, we're even. Everyone deep down is pretty disgusted w/ everyone else.

(You'd be proud, LJ, we are now "smoke free" in public buildings, restaurants, theaters, etc. It took a lot of protesting and dedicated people who felt as strongly as you.)

December 21, 1986, 1:30 AM

Struggling to make it thru the day when there is no struggle in sight. It comes from that place where no one, not even self, can see.

The Box is full...Jan 1 is near...Little Billy is lying on her back, Feet in the air, shadow boxing. Today for the first time she hopped up on the bed on her own. Now I'll never have any peace. She's smart, is getting a little better at her potty training but there are still daily messes to clean up. Mostly puddles, "Lake Billy's" I call them.

Went shopping today. Bought 12 pairs of sneaks (7 for Ma). They were 50% off. Averaged about $12.50 a pair. I hope this is an optimistic sign that I expect to live to wear them all out. I'm almost back down to my old weight of 155. It's amazing how anxiety cuts the appetite and tilts the scales.

I got out the only remaining key to my secret box upstairs and put Dr. Carson's name on it. I don't know exactly why, but I'd really like her to have them (journals), even if she never opens them or decides to torch them. I love and trust her enough to allow her to see all the nitty gritty embarrassing crap that would probably bore her. Gotta sleep, it's almost 2 AM.

ONE SMALL BOX

I put all of my life in a box
And it was not even full;
Some songs, a few pictures and poems,
Countless journals—all, one in the same,
A few pictures of people I loved
Some smiling—some not.
All My thoughts, feelings,
Hopes and dreams,
My failures and successes,
How sad to think
That all of them together
Could not even fill
One small box. LJE (Just thinking of me at RPC)

December 22, 1986, 12:30 AM

> **Observation LJE: Loneliness, the emptiness fills me, a void in itself yet total, encompassing all, revealing all. Nowhere to hide, no secret place. Nothing is without its vulnerability. Not even a tear has meaning. Each in shining singularity falls, origin unknown. Hopelessly I search for an answer.**

Went to my place again. I watch as the headlights come and go across the dark interior of my car and then once again it's just me and the music and the melancholy that never seems to depart…lately that is anyway, and though I know it hasn't always been this way and it won't be forever there is only right now and it is yesterday, now, and forever. Intellect can never convince the heart that what it feels is not an absolute truth. Pain has no middle ground and though I know what I'm feeling isn't really all that bad, it's like the steady drip…drip…drip that wears away the hardest stone. It can also drive ya crazy. So what seems like hardly anything can really be the proverbial "straw that breaks the camel's back" and those who look on in judgment will never find forgiveness, whereas those, who, in love, spare judgment, for them there is no fault. What I do is not a reflection on the strength of my love for my family and I believe they know this. It is a struggle I wage w/in myself to answer the un-answerable question "why?"

Like Billy Joel sings "You can't go the distance w/too much resistance." and here I sit exhausted, tired all the time at age 29 from 29 years of resisting all the way. Even what should have been, could have been easy, I have made hard. I've allowed countless projections to batter my head to a pulp as I see others w/critical eyes.

If they could only know how utterly exhausted I am, how I've tried my utmost not to hurt them; how I've hung on so many times just because of the strength of our love for each other. But if they knew, if they only knew how tired I am, maybe they could comprehend why I just want to go to sleep and never wake up. "No-thanks" to eternal life. Eternal nothingness will be fine thank you. I'd just as soon be dust, to be dust soon. But it's 3 days till Christmas eve and I have made promises…if only to myself. They are my family and they matter.

SNOW FALL

My prayer was a question
Lost in the silence
Of a new fallen snow; and though
I waited, shivering and fearful,
No answer came.

The sky did not rumble nor the
Stars twinkle with uncommon brilliance,
Only the snow falling gently against
My face, melting and flowing
Like tears, down a lonely gaze...
But then,
Like a warm breeze from within,
My heart lifted as the touch of a silent lover
Caressed my soul.

The moment faded and I wondered—
Had it been a dream?
Everything seemed the same:
The darkness, the night, the snow...
But as I took a step to leave,
Glancing down upon a flawless blanket of white,
I saw not one set of foot prints but,
Ever so close where a lover might have stood,
Was a second set of prints,
Neither coming nor going, only standing there
Close by my side.

LauraJo Engebrecht
Christmas 1986

December 25, 1986 2:15 AM

It was a struggle but I made it. Even had a good time last night with the Jacobsons. They are very nice people... I'm glad that it's all over (almost). Been taking aspirin so regularly that my ears are ringing. It's this damn headache. I've had it for a week. Just won't seem to go away.

My eyes hurt, my head hurts, my ears are ringing and my back hurts. I'm out of shape and fat and dieing doesn't seem all that bad just now.

December 27, 1986, Saturday, 12:45 AM

We all had a super time bowling tonight. Ten of us got 2 lanes and had a hysterical time of it. Jeff & Jodi, Kurt and Sue, Mom and Dad, the Jacobsons and me. Then we went to dinner at some Italian restaurant. It sure is a blessing to get along so well w/one's in-laws. Jeff is lucky.

As of tomorrow at 2 when the Jacobsons fly home to NJ I have fulfilled my weary commitment to try to be (not only present) but gracious and happy over the holidays. I guess I did OK at gracious--happy was kind of a bust. But I did try and in "being here" I succeeded.

Now I don't really know what I'll do. I'm pretty forlorn but I do believe if I can hang in, it'll get better. I really believe that.

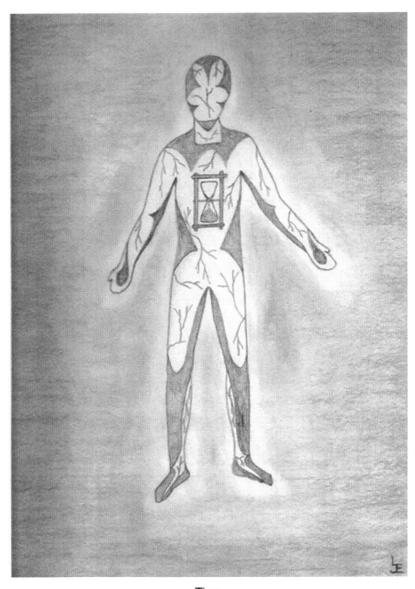

Time

BALANCE DESTROYED

I gave her my all
And she gave the same.
The scales are balanced,
With no one in debt.
But one side burns with a
Pain the other side will
Never know. It will
Destroy the balance,
Ending in separation and
Death, a death untimely,
A death without reason,
A death without purpose,
And no hand can catch
These sands which slip
Steadily away. LJE
(Thinking of Dr. C.)

December 28, 3 AM

Observation LJE: The clock ticks, the house sleeps yet I can't. There is too much running about upstairs and though silence prevails, the din is unbearable.

Trouble sleeping? Why do you ask???Exhausted and sleepless, what a combination.

Dr. C is leaving for California on the 4th thru the 26th. She's offered to leave me w/some phone #s, which is being her usual kind self.

You know what scares me most this time? It's getting caught too soon and going thru all that torture. I'd like them to get me soon enough to use any surviving organs. That at least would be a positive result of my death.

God I wish I could barf...I feel like I really need to and this is only from 3 pills...if I were to take them all they'd probably start coming up before I took the last one.

I've got a kind of psychological repulsion to taking pills these days. Can't imagine why! Tomorrow ought to be work as usual except for my 12:00 appt. w/Cecile. I hope to throw all this crap I have down the sewer tomorrow or at least before the new year. I refuse to enter a New Year carrying around the same old shit.

If I could throw them out I bet I'd be proud of myself...a simple little act dropping them thru the sewer grate and never looking back. Oh what a proud moment that would be, even all by myself. No helpers, no audience, just me, doing what is right. Tomorrow (today) we'll see what I'm made of.

Chapter Thirty-nine

Observation LJE: Thoughts are like sunsets. The majority hold common place beauty, but a few are memorably spectacular.

If the beauty of this world cannot ease my fears and sadness then I am hopeless, but w/joy and relief I say it does for only about 15 min ago I sat by the side of the road on my bike gazing out across the most beautiful landscape I'd seen since I last opened my eyes to one (for surely they are all around us every day; even the city has its sunsets and flowers). It was a picture of rolling hills in a spectrum of Mother Nature's summer colors and though the sun was hidden behind billowed thunderheads, fingers of light made a fan from heaven to earth and I was moved toward a higher order of priorities. What had worried me now seemed trite and soon disappeared altogether and though I had never doubted, I was reminded not only of God but of his undying, all giving love for me. I wished I had a camera so I could take this free beauty home w/me to keep forever but forever was already mine as it was written on my mind. The timeless scrapbook God gives each of us to keep if we will only take the time to stop and look…to stop and feel. He lets us fill it with the kind of pictures we choose to keep and when one page is filled there is always another just for the asking. I want to start filling my pages w/the loveliest of memories and to go even further by creating my own unturned future pages. I can see what will be and by seeing it makes it real so that someday the visions be- come the memories and I will feel more in control of my destiny than ever before in my life.

The pendulum slows w/time. Extremes grow closer and I know more so every day that I'll make it till His time not mine.

*This journal is an important and integral part to a series of such writings belonging to LauraJo Engebrecht and hav- ing been documented over the past 8-10 years. In event of my decease, it will become the property of:

Dr. Cecile Carson, M.D.
Rochester, N.Y. 14607

Along with the entire collection contained in a small brown wooden chest I have constructed and which is located at my current residence (and if not there, then with my parents). It is locked and there is only one key. Its where abouts are revealed somewhere in this journal. (Note: Also included is sketch pad and writing pad with poems. Please leave everything intact.) My hopes are that some scien- tific knowledge may be gained into the mystery of chronic depression and anxiety. I also leave my body for psycho- scientific research w/in the same areas. Signed: LauraJo Engebrecht 5/19/85

Dr. Cecile Carson, M.D.
8-31-10

I am an internist and counselor and was LauraJo Engebrecht's doctor from November 4, 1983 until her death in January, 1987. We began our work together when she was referred to me by her psychiatrist for medical clearance before prescribing a medication.

Our next contact was April 9, 1985, following a psychiatric discharge after an overdose of a warfarin rat poison. In a style and pattern that would repeat over the next several years, she both felt better and was planning her next suicide attempt. With her talent, compassion, and exquisite sensitivity and articulation through poetry, song and writing, it was difficult to accept she had a potentially lethal illness. Her mental health diagnosis, termed "borderline personality disorder" required a strong team of support—her psychiatrist and myself medically, and her very strong family support. This disorder is characterized by impulsivity, and of no strong sense of self, and suicide attempts. I knew that so many things had been tried before—counseling, medication and prolonged instatutialization—that I decided to keep an open mind about what was possible. I had a long-standing interest in complementary and alternative medicine (called at that time "holistic health"), and I wondered if any of this might be helpful.

We tried some deep hypnosis and found that she was "divided." One part, focused on her left side, was called "Laura" and was the child aspect of herself that was angry/rebellious/abusive. She awoke one night to find her left hand choking herself. LauraJo also new there was a strong part of her that did not want to die and that fought

"Laura" off. As she became more agitated over the next few months, she felt less safe in doing this kind of work, so we discontinued trying to resolve the two aspects of herself through this means.

LauraJo and I had an easy rapport; she felt safe saying whatever she needed to, that I would not judge her, but listen as carefully as I could. She brought in a poem she wrote one day that spoke of her feelings about this:

The Gambler's Hand

I do not share my words with many,
Fearing they won't understand.
I hold them close like a gambler's cards
Keeping my ace close at hand.
But with you, I have no need to hide.
I will show you every card.
For you are kind when the world is cruel,
And soft when the world is hard.

Between late 1985 and early 1986 she was relatively stable and made no attempts to harm herself, but in May of 1986, she ingested 10 bags of rat poison and overdosed on an antidepressant, requiring an intensive care admission to monitor whether the absence of brain wave activity was permanent or temporary. A conversation with her mother in the ICU waiting room during that time haunted me. With great compassion and sadness she said, "I'm not sure we're doing her a favor." I certainly realized that medically

I was doing the right thing, but knew that bringing her back would also continue the deep suffering that dwelled deep inside. I also remember vividly one of her suicide attempts, and I use it in teaching doctors in training about the way in which we are connected to our patients in more than the usual ways. I have written it as a brief case study:

It is 3:00 a.m. and I am awakened suddenly from deep sleep by an image of my patient LJ drifting out into the cosmos. Inexplicably, I go downstairs in my home and sit in meditation for a few minutes, finding myself saying, "LJ come back: come on back," over and over again. I then go upstairs to bed and to sleep.

I find out a week later from an angry LJ that she had once again tried to kill herself, this time with an amount of medication which she calculated to be twice the minimum lethal dose listed in a toxicology text. She was shocked to find herself alive the following morning. She reported taking the pills around 11:00 p.m. the night I had been awakened. She carried the diagnosis of borderline personality disorder, had been quite unstable, and had been working with both her psychiatrist and me as her internist. There had been no inkling of her plan at our last visit 2 weeks previously; nor any contact between us by phone or message.

In LauraJo's pattern of "cycling," there were definitely some positive things she would do that would help herself during an "up" phase: working, volunteering, making a new friend, finding a church group, riding her motorcycle, making her art. Yet it seemed that the deep place in her that was the source of her suffering and her uncertainty would always emerge from its darkness into the light of day. No amount of cognitive understanding could change it. I felt that the most important thing that I and others could do was to create as strong a safety net of loving support as possible. And yet, LauraJo would cry about feeling that she was caught on a merry-go-round of wanting to live and wanting to die—and that part of the trap was love and caring from others who she felt she would hurt (and who hurt with her whether or not she attempted to harm herself, because they understood her struggles),

LauraJo and I would occasionally use a barter system to pay for some of her visits to me. She had a beautiful, simple style of making small sculptures of people and animals that expressed volumes in a single line of the clay. Most were very positive: a mother kneeling and holding a child, a friend sitting next to someone with a hand on the person's back, a healer bending over someone who was ill. Once she brought a small, but magnificent eagle with one wing furled. The other wing was outstretched—but full of holes, and it was clear the eagle would never fly. It broke my heart to see it, as I felt she was giving me a clear message.

In September of 1986, we transferred her internal medicine care to Dr. Don Symer, and I continued on in a counseling role for her. Over the next few months, LauraJo seemed to become more remote in terms of her attachment to this life and I began to fear that she would end up with a successful suicide. In November, she returned after an overdose of medication after accidently running over and killing her beloved dog. During that same time, a friend of hers had overdosed on medication and died.

We also met a week later after this attempt, and the major issue for her was realizing that death would not solve the deeper issue she felt she was struggling with—that death is not the escape hatch she thought. Although she got a new dog a week later, on December 30 she once again overdosed and required hospitalization and being put on a respirator. At this point, I felt great sadness being with her in the hospital; at a deep level I felt she was letting go of the struggle to try to live in this world.

On January 1, 1987, she was successful in her leave-taking. I don't know why I didn't awaken from sleep once again to call her back; I will always wonder if some part of me unconsciously colluded to let her go.

Shortly after her death, I took the small eagle off my shelf. I had planned to use it in teaching medical students about compassion, about mental health disorders. But I felt something more important needed to be done with it. I did not want to hold LauraJo in that image of suffering and not being able to fly. She HAD "flown," and I wanted to have instead an image of her great flight into the next phase of her soul. So I placed it carefully in a burlap bag, took out a sledgehammer and pounded it back into the original clay of the earth. I buried it in my back yard, asking the Earth to absorb and transform all that pain and suffering she had endured as a final release.

As a physician, I know that patients come to us as our greatest teachers. LauraJo has been one of those for me, and I'm grateful to have walked part of her path with her.

An Instant (Optional title–Dr. C.) LJE

She touched my heart
She saw a blur of my soul
And I loved her in an instant,
But the end was already written
And could not be changed
Not even her love...
Or whatever it was,
Was enough
And though I loved her deeply,
She won't miss me long
When I'm gone,
For the depth of love
Must have a reflection
To be lasting.
(Sunday 5/18/85 7:15 PM at RPC...thinking of
those I've loved deeply)

FREE

The captured eagle
Shall be free
On winds uplifted
O'er the sea.
On loves light wings
She'll rise and soar
Returning to earth
Nevermore.

Mourn not her absence,
Meant to be.
Look to the heavens
You will see
Her waiting there
To ease your way
Turning darkness
To light of day.

"Together - Alone"
By LauraJo Engebrecht

Lord, what would be the consequences
For taking my own life?
What would be my punishment for
Ending this ceaseless strife?

Would I be forced to witness, Lord
My potential glory,
To see the friends I could have had
Throughout my life's story?

Trading one hell for another
Is all my death would be.
But here the pain is familiar
Change is risky to me.

So I've decided to stay here
Together and alone
Until my Lord says it's o.k.
For me to come on home.

Even though, through all your hospitalizations, my talks to you about living for yourself, not us, even my request to Dr. Carson to *let you go,* I felt nothing but disbelief—the "NO!" ringing, echoing within me when the policeman stood at our door on that first wintry day of 1987. He was tall, I think. I really don't remember. ".....early morning discovery in Powder Mill Park.....charcoal in a pie pan.....music on the stereo." And you were gone.

1970's Tennis Star Apparent Suicide
LauraJo Engebrecht found dead in car in Powder Mill Park

The front page headlines, pictures of your playing and winning tennis days. The story touches briefly on your life, your struggles, your family. How cold and hollow, so impersonal the facts seem... you were and now you are no more. The telephone rings.

Kurt and I chose to see you. Your father and Jeff declined. Your hair, that corn silk color curled softly around your face, so peaceful, almost a half-smile and I knew you had arrived home safely. I gave thanks for the soft sleep of Carbon Monoxide...no horror of vomiting, internal bleeding, convulsions...just the quiet slumber of death.

BJ mourned your death with us. She curled up on your bed and only with coaxing would she come down. She was so young. She became your father's dog after you left, LJ. As long as she lived, your presence was magnified for we knew that you had left her for us to share your love.

The trunk with its contents was given to Dr. Carson who returned it to us within the year of your death. We did not know of your wishes to donate your body, thus you were cremated and your ashes spread at your favorite waterfall with little Roo's.

Ironically, LJ, that last note I received from you was pinned to the verse on the calendar that admonished us to *live*.

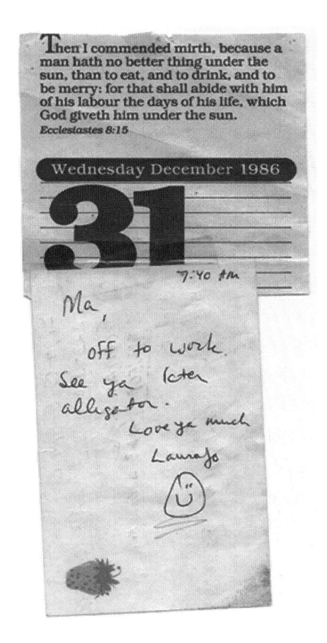

Where were you in your journey when you wrote the following thoughts on life? You believed.

LIFE'S SUBSTANCE

Something of life
Unyielding to lens
Or brush refuses to
Be laid down, interpreted
By patterned, colored dots.
The sparkle of new snow,
A weightless, dancing leaf
In autumn. The ripples on
A glass-like pond. The
Grace of a stalking cat, the
Moon rising huge and orange
Over the hill.
The anguish, the joy, the
Subtle delicacy of life make
More than a picture, more
Than a poem. It is an art
In itself, ever changing
Ever reaching to us saying
Live…live…live!

Although you could not, I believe this is the message you wanted to leave to all those who find themselves sharing your journey.

Chapter Forty

Not being church goers, our neighbor offered to speak to her minister, Reverend Kent Garner. Kurt handled the notice to the paper, the program for our friends, your friends.

Funeral of LauraJo Engebrecht Delivered by Reverand Kent Garner speaking for LJ, our family and friends:

January 5, 1987

We gather this morning to remember and celebrate the life of LauraJo Engebrecht. We gather with a variety of emotions, coming from a variety of places…for we all process grief differently, we all face death uniquely. Our emotions are even more intense this morning because of Laura's youth. The young aren't supposed to die; we can't rationalize their death, comfort ourselves with thoughts of long and full lives. And even further complicating our emotions today is the fact that Laura's death is a suicide-that she is responsible for her own death, that on the surface at least there was some choice. And so we come bearing our own baggage, our own pain, our own thoughts.

What can we say this morning? Is there any way to make sense out of what seems so senseless? Our tendency is to find cause, to fix blame, to explain actions and then up with the "answers"...at least that fit our needs at the moment. I don't have any easy answers; I'm not sure there ARE any answers. But in the midst of our questions, we can find some comfort.

LauraJo was a remarkably talented person. Gifted athlete, sensitive musician, creative designer. She excelled at many things. She had a personable way—especially with people older than herself. She had a knack at communicating with them. She was a vital partner in a very close family. She won tennis championships; she won a furniture design and construction while still in high school. She loved music – had great talent with music. And she had a relationship with God...that she developed on her own, that was not inherited, but was born out of her own struggles, needs and joys. She had much going for her. But she also had a great handicap working against her: An uneasiness with life, a compulsion toward death. We can look for causes—we recognized certain symptoms after the flood in the Basin. Yet I am not sure we will ever find the cause...if there was a cause. Those of you who loved her have played most of the "guilt games" there are to play--could we have done more, should we have been more restrictive; but we have (thankfully, I think) come to the realization that although perhaps we could have done more ...we could never have done enough.

That Laura's needs were insatiable, her insecurity endless. Laura had an illness—that's hard for us to under stand. Because we could not diagnose it, define it, name it, contain it, control it…we had trouble understanding it, no less treating it. It wasn't as if she could Try harder not to want to die…any more than a cancer patient could try harder not to die. And even more insidious, Laura knew all this about her disease, about herself. At one time she actually said: "You know, if I had cancer and fought this hard and this long, I would be a hero!" We could have, I guess, placed her in an institution for the rest of her life… for it appears that this was a life-long, incurable disease. On the surface, that looks like it might have been the most loving thing to do. But, in reality, that would have been a sentence to death…with no chance for life, a death that would take a life-time to occur. By offering Laura freedom, we offered her a chance for life…even in the context of death. It was a courageous decision by her family, and I believe a loving decision, to give her this freedom.

Laura taught us much in her life. She taught us sensitivity, the value of expressing our feelings. In spite of her illness, maybe because of her illness, we were forced to talk, to share, to emote. As we each spoke of our frustrations, we began to recognize the other's feelings. As we spoke of death and were threatened by death and learned to live with death, we began to understand life…and the value of life.

Laura taught us to laugh…sometimes at ourselves, sometimes in spite of herself, such as the time she went to Niagara Falls, and we didn't know "what" she had in mind, or if she would return…and she called from the thruway in tears: a tire had come off her car, and her comment was: "I could have been killed!" We had to laugh in spite of ourselves.

Laura taught us much. She taught us much about accepting each other...she taught us much about forgiving each other. I hope and pray that we never forget these lessons... or the one who taught them to us. But living on the edge for so long, living with this threat over us for so long, tends to harden us too...and make us callous to individual needs and unique circumstances—makes us critical of those who have not experienced so much—makes us cynical of those who don't understand/can't accept us. This would negate so much of what Laura taught us, and diminish the intensity with which she loved us.

Laura had a handicap: she somehow couldn't process and integrate her gifts, her accomplishments, her "self." She thought she was doing us and the world a favor by leaving us/by dying. She knew she had a sickness; but she could see no hope of help, no hope for health. And she took the only course she saw open to her.

We don't agree with her decision...but we accept it and it does nothing to diminish her love...and the love that we feel. Our comfort and our cause for celebration this day is that her struggle is over, that her long hard journey, her courageous fight—for each day was a fight to overcome all that would pull her down—her courageous fight finished, and she has ultimately found that elusive peace she so desperately sought. She is with the Lord she dearly loved and gave herself to...in a place where all tears are wiped away and grief is no more.

We thank God for her life among us. Her gifts to us. The growth she helped us achieve.

These gifts are precious...and we cling to them. We ask God to give us courage for the days ahead—to recognize around us those things for which Laura so desperately searched: life, love, relationships, beauty, hope, peace.

By our affirming her values...we affirm her, and hold her memory dear among us.

We ask God to care for our child, our sister, our friend... to give her eternal peace. We ask God to touch us. To sustain us with his grace and goodness...and peace...for we struggle with her death...even as we celebrate her life!

AMEN

So young—twenty-nine—over ten years of courageous struggle. But, LJ, only you could sing at your own funeral. We felt your story, your struggle was best told by you in your own words, own voice and so the poignancy of your pain and loneliness echoed throughout the church ending with a triumphant duet with your brother, Kurt "Amazing Grace!" So be it.

Reflections to you, LJ, my family and friends

Twenty plus years have passed. Nine grandchildren grace our celebrations and I regale them with tales of you, their Aunt LauraJo. When they ask how you died, I tell them. I speak of your courage, your daring, your compassion but most of all I share with them your gift of love and acceptance.

The end? Is there ever an end to love no matter how flawed? Love has no boundaries, no rights, or wrongs. Love is.

So why, after these twenty plus years do I read your journals, suffer again through the tortuous twists and turns of your struggle from inside your heart and soul? Wasn't my own journey enough? But the journals are all numbered as if in preparation for this story, this sharing with some other troubled soul who might see a glimmer of light from your darkness, to know they are not alone.

And so it is **for you** I have shared your journals with those who question life. Throughout your struggle, there was always some moment, laughter echoes, some small adventure that made it worthwhile, and I feel privileged to have shared those moments with you. I know you want to assure all those victims of mental illness, their parents, spouses, brothers, sisters, and friends, whose life's drama is tied together in love, who hold on through the tortuous struggle with unnamed demons, those who watch their loved one succumb to a self-destructive death, to *know* that they could not have prevented it. The mystery of life eludes us all, LJ. You would be the first to advise your fellow travelers to be kind to themselves, to know and *believe* that they have done and are doing the best they can.

As the years move on, I find the days pass more quickly and sometimes I wonder how much control we actually have over our destiny. If the creative tools of life are indeed: *thought, word, and deed,* does that mean that every turn of our life's path reflect an action we have taken from choices we have made?

I truly believe that each of us holds the seed for eternity in the love we share today. As Deepak Chopra notes in *Reinventing the Body, Resurrecting the Soul*, "It's the universe's task to unfold reality; yours is only to plant the seed."

Although I have just discovered the following song, and I never heard you sing it…you always made your love for your father and me very evident…you planted many seeds of love in your life.

Shining Ways (from LJ's 1985 note pad)

I never wrote you a song before because
I couldn't find the words to say
How much your love means to me
Every moment of everyday.
From baby stroller to roller skates
Then from tricycles on to cars,
You let me learn I was worthy of life
Helped me reach for my inner most stars.
You taught me right from wrong and more.
You showed me just what you meant
Thru (your) lives of loving and giving,
I've no doubt you were heaven sent.

I travel my road as a woman now
With one (very) special thing to say
That any good I may do in my life
Is a reflection of your (shining) ways.
You gave me life on a (warm) summer day
Loved me and made me strong
You are my father and mother
And for you I sing this song

The passages I have selected from your journals are but a small etching of your art, thoughts, observations, and feelings. I have placed your journals back into your chest with your letters, drawings, photos and awards to be carried lovingly wherever I go. Your generosity and love touched people wherever you went. Following is a poem sent to us by Ginger and Basil Michels from Brook Hollow:

TO THE PARENTS

"I'll lend you for a little while a child of Mine," He said,
"For you to love the while she lives and mourn for when she's dead.
It may be six or seven or twenty-two or three,
But will you till I call for her, take care of her for Me?
She'll bring her charms to gladden you and shall her stay be brief,
You'll have her lovely memories as solace for your grief.

I cannot promise she will stay since all from earth return,
But there are lessons taught down there I want this child to learn.
I've looked the wide world over in My search for teachers true,
And from the throngs that crowd life's lane I have selected you.
Now will you give her all your love nor think the labor vain,
Nor hate Me when I come to call to take her back again?

I fancied that I heard you say, 'Dear Lord, Thy will be done.
For all the joy Thy child shall bring the risk of grief I'll run.
I'll shelter her with tenderness; I'll love her while I may
And for the happiness I've known forever grateful stay.
But should the angels call for her much sooner than we planned,
I'll bear the bitter grief that comes and try to understand.'"
(Anonymous)

LauraJo In Memory of her Life June 20, 1957–January 1, 1987

Like a song she lived among us
Her music, her art, her laughter, her wit
Brightened our lives.

Like a child she faced the world
Defenseless, open and scared.
And it was the pain, the suffering, the inequality
That filled her mind.

What she found was God,
The light in her darkness.
Through all her pain and loneliness
He was always there for her. Now she is with Him.

Why, you may ask, would one with so many gifts
Find so little joy in this world?
This is the essence of LJ's illness.
No matter the accomplishment, the love, the beauty
She received no sense of fulfillment from life.

As if clinging to a rope that spanned an abyss
She inched forward holding on to the thread of life.
At times she lost hope
But angels from everywhere came to her aid.

Her love, her strength and her hope
That someday a floor would somehow rise to save her
Gave her courage to share her life with us.

And now, all of us who have loved you
Send a message through our Lord
Bursting into heaven like a wind through the wintry night
Thank you, LauraJo, for all you have given us.

After living so long in pain only to give us joy,
We celebrate and rejoice in your long deserved peace.
K.H.E

EPILOGUE

You gave yourself away by bits and pieces until there was nothing left and you could not live with the emptiness in your heart.

The Gambler
When all but the dealer
Have tired of the game,
He too must stop
Or play solitaire LJE

Is life a gift or a sentence? You chose sentence, LJ, I choose gift, and my greatest gift of all is the life I shared with you. I choose to celebrate this gift of time–the failures, the successes, the laughter, the tears. I see the light in your yellow-green, tiger eyes that were round as saucers, absorbing the wonders of life; and I give thanks for those memories. I see you on your motorcycle with little Roo, a bandanna tied over his large, rabbit-like ears tucked into the front of your leather jacket, the two of you riding with the wind and I know you are celebrating life just beyond the veil through which I cannot see but sense in my heart.

I end this saga with my favorite saying of yours:

LIVING IN THE LIGHT

The sun comes up every
Morning and though it
May be cloudy, each of us
Alone has the choice
Whether to acknowledge its
Presence, feel its warmth
Live in its light.
LJE

Pat's Publishing

Books by Pat

Chronicles of LauraJo When Love is Not Enough *
CreateSpace.com/3605803
Copyright 2012 by Pat Engebrecht

Under the Haystack
CreateSpace.com/3850853
Copyright 1973 by P.A. Engebrecht

Promise of Moonstone
CreateSpace.com/3850856
Copyright 1983 by Pat Engebrecht

* *CD When Love is Not Enough*
CreateSpace.com/2024149
Copyright 2012 by Pat Engebrecht

All books available as Kindle-eBook
Books available on Kindle ebooks on Amazon.com

Web page: www.patengebrecht.com

Borderline Personality Disorder Demystified
Robert O. Friedel, MD
www.bpddemystified.com

Jacquiline Gibb www.mentalhealtheducationfoundation.com

Made in the USA
Columbia, SC
14 May 2020